CLIMBING TURNS

Climbing Turns

A Pilot's Story in Peace and War

by

GROUP CAPTAIN

Patrick Foss

O B E

PUBLISHED IN 1990
BY LINDEN HALL
223 PRESTON ROAD, YEOVIL,
SOMERSET BA20 2EW

ISBN 0 948747 06 4
COVER DESIGN BY W. CAMERON JOHNSON
PRINTED IN MALTA BY INTERPRINT

Dedication

I dedicate this book to my wife Margaret, to our son Andrew, daughter Phoebe, her husband Christopher and our grandchildren Josephine and Thomas.

I wrote this book for them. Also for those who have asked me

> What did you do in the war?
>
> What was it like in those days?
>
> Do you really think an ordinary chap can affect history?

Acknowledgements

I want to express my great gratitude to my Californian friend Basil Entwistle, a skilled editor and writer, who gave so many hours to the shaping of this book. His enthusiasm, and his wife's enthusiasm, along with that of my family, brought the book to a finish.

I wish to thank John Faber and Vera Frampton who have done a major work preparing for the printing, to Bill Cameron Johnson for his cover design, Henry Macnicol, Daphne Waterston, Sylvia Waymouth and Margaret Baker for all their help. Most of all, thanks to my brother Denis for publishing the book.

Contents

List of Illustrations

List of Illustrations

1

Sea and Air

From a young age I recognised that my Mother was a remarkable woman, but that did not make it any easier to live with her. Her maiden name was Winifred Exton, from a Bournemouth family. She was known to everyone as 'Winkle'. My earliest recollections are of her managing a 120-bedroom hotel in Bournemouth, on England's south coast. She ran it very firmly and the staff of about sixty seemed a little scared of her. She ran me and my two brothers in much the same way. 'You walk on the sides of the corridor carpets,' she said to us,' the middle is for the guests to walk on.' If any of us heard a bell ring in the staff room, we listened. If it rang a second time one of us would run back there to find out why it had not been answered.

In those days Mother was a very masculine figure, with bobbed hair and a bow tie. But later I came to understand that behind that façade she was deeply insecure. Before she faced the crowded dining room she needed several Martinis. She smoked forty cigarettes a day. She must have inherited from her father some of his restless energy. He had come to Bourne-

mouth from Lincolnshire because of his delicate
health. While getting ready to die, however, he had
opened two hotels and several other businesses.
Mother as a girl liked to be regarded as 'sporty and
modern'. One night, for example, she swam out for
more than half a mile to surprise friends who were
sleeping on a yacht.

My father made far less impression on my life.
William Foss, the son of a solicitor in Croydon, was
handsome and witty and had swept Mother off her
feet. Their marriage broke up in 1920, when I was
seven. My most vivid memory of him is his sudden
appearance in my bedroom one evening wearing a gas
mask. It was his new toy, brought from the World War
I officer training course he was taking. He had meant
it as a joke, but it threw me into panic and nightmares
for years afterwards.

Father went to school at Eastbourne College and on
to Cambridge, where he gained a half-Blue for running, but no degree. In some ways that typified his
life. At the University he became a Fabian socialist,
much influenced by H.G. Wells, Bertrand Russell and
the family Webb. The best man at his wedding was
Hugh Dalton, later to become a Labour Chancellor of
the Exchequer. Father for a while devoted himself to
the theatre. He launched two plays in London and
both failed - one of them opened a few days before
the outbreak of World War I, which closed all theatres
- an expensive misjudgement.

Mother told me that she was summoned as a
defendant to the High Court in London, where she
was sued as guarantor for the expenses of the play.

She denied to me that she had signed the document and claimed her signature was forged, but she could not plead that in court without incriminating her husband. So her defence was that she had signed within ten days of giving birth and was not competent.

During the war Father got temporary work resettling Belgian refugees in England. Then he went to Trinidad in the West Indies to work at extracting pitch. He had to leave because of complaints about his relations with company wives. He then went into officer training, but the war ended before he was ready for France. He had lived way beyond his means, leaving his new wife to fend for herself and the children.

Mother had hated that court appearance and the chicanery involved. Five years later, Father asked her to divorce him, which meant further court appearances, publicity and notoriety. She hated Father for it. For sixteen years of my youth he was never mentioned in our home. My brothers and I did not know if he was alive or dead. I was in my twenties when I began to enquire about Father and learned to my surprise that he had been a Parliamentary reporter for the *Morning Post* and a dramatic critic; that he had written a controversial book on the life of Franco of Spain; that he had been married and divorced three times. In World War II he was working as a sorter in a post office in South London, living alone, when a German bomb fell on his lodgings and killed him.

When I was at boarding school I realised that I hated him. I told myself that it was because he had walked out and left Mother with three children and no support. She had had to work long and hard to bring us up. It was much later that I saw that my hatred arose from my shame over the marriage break-up, which did not permit me to talk about my father or family as other boys could. The thing that determined me the most was the adamant desire not to be beholden to my mother and to stand, as quickly as I could, on my own feet and earnings.

I was born in Ketton, Rutland, on 8 November 1913 - I never discovered why Mother happened to be there. My parents were frequently on the move, from friends to friends; they ran up debts and moved on to avoid creditors. Hannen was born in Hertfordshire less than a year after me, and Denis in Southbourne, near Bournemouth, eighteen months later. Mother also took on fostering a girl, Jane, whose mother had died and whose father was at the war. By that time Mother had been given work running the Linden Hall Hotel, Bournemouth, by her brother Leo and the family, which enabled her to provide a home for her children. Mother had 'modern' ideas about bringing up children. Running a big hotel gave her little time to spend with her sons, so she installed us in a house near the hotel and hired a cook and a nurse to look after us. We went to a nearby kindergarten. Later she decided we needed a tutor, so she placed an advertisement in a paper, 'Wanted - a couple to look after three young boys. House with all expenses and small salary.' Next day, when she came down for breakfast in the hotel she found the drive filled with couples. For weeks afterwards, hundreds more applied. Mother took the head porter to an upper bedroom window, pointed out the ones she thought looked suitable, sent Mr Cherry down to bring them in and tell the rest that she was 'suited'. From that haphazard selection came Captain Marples.

Marples had been a rubber planter in Malaya who had brought a battalion of Chinese pioneers to France in World War I. After the war he had lost his planting job and came to England seeking work at a time of major unemployment. He had recently married. He proved to be a marvellous man for boys and we loved him.

He taught us manners and gave us a great interest in games and hobbies, both indoor and out. Mah Jong was one of our favourites. If he found one of us idle he would detail him to sentry duty outside the front gate with a broomstick. When a visitor or tradesman approached, he was to be challenged with a 'Who goes there?' When bona fides were established they were to be paid the proper courtesies by our presenting arms. This was soon after World War I and everyone was amused. When I was nine, Mother sent us to boarding school and Marples became assistant bursar in a private school.

Twice a week Mother had us for dinner in the hotel dining room. She insisted we dress up for it, take a glass of wine with the meal and a small cigar with coffee. Friends suggested to her that this would encourage us to smoke and drink as adults. However, none of us smoked and I was the only one who drank to excess, when I was an RAF officer.

Mother encouraged us to bring her a present before the meal. I discovered that she was pleased to accept

the recitation of a limerick. I can still recall many of
them. A favourite was:

> At beauty I am not a star
> There are others more handsome by far.
> But my face I don't mind it
> For I am behind it.
> It's the people in front get the jar.

Mother tried out most of the fashionable religions
of the day - the one she stayed longest with was
Spiritualism. Several of her best friends were practi-
tioners, including Hannen Swaffer, the writer and
journalist after whom my brother Hannen was named.
But she found in none of these beliefs a cure for her
bitterness towards Father, nor release from her forty
cigarettes a day. And she held strong views about 'not
stuffing religion' down the throats of children.

On Sundays Mother used to come to the school to
take us out, and so we avoided having to attend
church and learn the collect for the day. She kept a
set of the books of Havelock Ellis and encouraged us
to read them because she felt we should know all
about sex and perversions.

When I was about nine years old I decided I wanted
to go to sea in the Merchant Navy. I searched a
reference book of schools and found the Nautical
College, Pangbourne. Mother agreed she would send
me there, when I was thirteen. Hannen went to
Canford School and Denis followed me to Pangbourne.

At the end of my first year, aged fourteen, I spent my summer vacation signing-on a tramp steamer on the run from Cardiff to Oporto in Portugal as a shilling-a-month steward. I slept and ate in the officers' quarters, but did any work that needed doing, from scraping paint to taking a turn at the steering wheel. When I was seasick the Captain sent me down to the engine room where I was put to work greasing the steel piston rods as they reciprocated out of the cylinders. It was at that point in the ship where the movements were minimal.

On our second day at sea I confidently offered to assist the Captain with the navigation. We must have been well out in the Bay of Biscay. He took a sun sight with a sextant, worked out his position and marked the chart. Then he invited me to use his sextant reading and do my own calculation. I used the Marc St Hilaire method taught us at Pangbourne and also marked the chart. There was a difference of about twenty miles, about two and a half hours steaming for this old ship. The Captain was taken aback by my brash confidence. He examined my calculations, which were double dutch to him, while I dismissed his workings as straight out of the ark. He sucked his teeth, looked through the bridge house door at a tramp wallowing a mile away and said, 'If he's there, I'm there,' pointing to his plot. 'When do you estimate we'll reach Finisterre, sir?' (The northernmost point of Spain.) 'Noon tomorrow,' he replied. Next morning I was put to chipping paint on the forecastle. The Captain was on the bridge, looking out for Finisterre from eleven o'clock onward. We reached the Cape around three in the afternoon.

A year later I signed on for another trip with my brother Denis, this time from Barry Docks in South Wales to Nantes on the River Loire in France, conveying coal dust to a power station. We came home empty, like an enormous cork on the sea. When we shipped a hard wave over the bows some hatch covers were stove in, letting sea into the empty hold. The crew rushed to cover it, but the pumps could not shift the water because the outlets were choked with coal dust. Denis and I and others were sent down with spikes to clear the strum boxes, which looked like beehives with many small holes in them.

The water in the hold was breast-high and as the ship rolled the water rushed from side to side, with black scum on its surface, slamming large timbers against the sides of the hold. We had to take a deep breath, note where the timbers were headed, duck under the surface, stab madly at the strum boxes to free their holes and hope the bone crushing timbers would miss us. Before long the pumps began to pull and the water level fell. We climbed on deck, feeling lucky to be alive, and were met by a stream of icy water from the mate's hose as he sprayed off the coal dust. After that the mugs of cocoa never tasted so good.

As we came into Barry Docks the Captain said to me, 'See that ship over there, the *Clan McX*. Every man on her has an officer's ticket, even the deckhands, stokers and greasers.' At that moment I glimpsed dimly the dimension of the vast unemployment grip-

ping the country - something like two million registered. Those were the early days of the Great Depress-
ion. Then and there I decided that for an ambitious
lad like me the sea was not my profession.

My thoughts turned to the sky, and when Hannen
wrote from his school about a rising aircraft designer,
a Mr Miles, who had given a lecture, I wrote Miles
asking him how I might get into aviation. His reply
was encouraging: get all the instruction I could in
engineering (Pangbourne had an engineering department) and the use of tools, pass my exams well and
then seek an apprenticeship with a good aircraft
manufacturing firm. I remained at Pangbourne just
long enough to pass the School Certificate, surprising
myself by getting four credits. Then I applied to
Saunders Roe, flying boat constructors on the Isle of
Wight, enlisting an uncle to recommend me for a
premium apprenticeship. Like so many other companies, Saunders Roe had almost no work. They said
they would notify me when they had an opening.

While waiting, I worked at a garage near the hotel.
I pumped petrol into the customers' cars, I ground in
valves, I helped skilled men work on jobs and learned
a lot. I was not paid - no one in those days expected
to be paid for learning a trade. I felt sure that I was
headed on my chosen road of aviation.

Before Christmas Mother said to me, 'I'll want you
home over the holidays to help in the hotel. You can
take on the issuing of stores and the routine purchasing. You can also look after the dances in the evenings.'
I protested, 'I can't dance.' 'What do I hire a dance
hostess for?' said Mother. 'Go and see Vera and tell

her you want to learn to dance.' I did so and it was not long before I became a confident dancer.

In due course I became sufficiently skilled to demonstrate the latest slow foxtrot, with an excellent partner, to an admiring ballroom. This did nothing to lessen my ego. It dawned on me that many girls came to the hotel on holiday looking for an interesting man. I learnt that if I was considerate to a girl's mother, she would encourage me to be nice to her daughter, even financing me for it. I began to build up an array of girls, each of whom thought that I was their special, and hoped I felt the same way. Whenever I got too involved I would salve my conscience with the thought that next week she would be gone. But there came a Christmas when six girl friends came to the hotel, each expecting to be treated as Number One. I did not want rows, nor to lose business for the hotel. My solution was to make a dead set for a girl I had not met before, undeniably the prettiest in the place. All six girls were mortified at first, but had to concede that with that smasher as competition, they could understand my losing my head.

Then came the next step along the aviation path. A young aviation engineer visited the hotel. He told me that if I wanted to learn to fly, the most inexpensive way was to go to Germany where I could get cheap flying instruction, especially on gliders, because of the high rate of exchange of the Travellers Mark. I wrote at once to book myself for the first course in the spring on the Wasserkuppe in Bavaria. I found someone who would give me lessons in German in the evenings. Then I went to Mother and told her of the advantages of learning the language in Germany. She asked how much it would cost. I gave her a price which would include the flying instruction, though I did not mention that. She agreed. At some point she realised the reason for my going, but to her credit she neither made an issue of it, nor showed fear. How many mothers in those days would have allowed a sixteen-year-old son to go to a foreign country without even a knowledge of the language to learn to fly?

After a long rail journey down the Rhine and into the hinterland I reached the mountain, Wasserkuppe, upon which the gliding school stood. I found a number of German youth milling around the station and we clubbed together to hire a taxi. The school consisted of long, low army huts, divided into small rooms sleeping two each. Other huts were a dining room, cook house and workshops, with hangars alongside. The whole place was under several feet of snow and a blanket of fog. There was no possibility of gliding. We were given some ground instruction and sat around and filled the day as best we could. I found two Britishers on the course, one a dance band drummer in his mid-thirties and the other a student aged twenty-one.

For a week the fog and snow continued and we hung around very frustrated as our course seemed to be slipping away. The tension grew and there was a good deal of riotous talk and some heavy drinking. One day the drummer said to me, 'They don't know it, but I understand some German. These chaps are planning to "scalp" our British student. While I've no use for him, we've got to defend him. Are you on?' I felt scared, but agreed. That evening two of the German students, who had been friendly, invited me to have a drink and learn some of their songs. They plied me with drinks until I passed out and they put me to bed. Some others did the same to my drummer friend. The student had been aware of trouble and had barricaded himself in his room. The rioters began to break down his door.

At the height of the furore the student's German room mate, unaware of the plot, came down the corridor. He seized a chair leg and, starting from the back, proceeded to lay men out one by one. After a furious fight the room mate leaped out of a window and disappeared into the night, followed by the student and chased by the others. Next morning the camp authorities searched for the two, found them and brought them back. Several Germans were dismissed and order was restored. Hours later, the weather broke, the sun melted the snow and we were all overjoyed when the flying training started.

In 1931, Germany led the world in the art of gliding. This was no accident. Under the Versailles Treaty, following World War I, the country was forbidden to train military pilots. Men who looked ahead to the building of an air force used gliding to create a reservoir of men skilled in the basics of flying. We pupils started by sitting on a glider pointed into a brisk wind, trying to keep it level by moving the control column which operated the ailerons on the wing ends. Next we slithered along the ground. Then we were catapulted a few feet into the air above a gentle slope to glide down, keeping the craft level and parallel to the slope. It was all solo work, learning by trial and error. The instructor shouted instructions, but in the end the pilot himself had to find the feel of the controls and work them. Our first goal was to gain the 'A' licence - controlled flight in a straight line for one minute. That took most of us about a week.

To catapult the glider the instructor stood at a wing end, holding it level, while a team of four men held a V of rubber rope stretched from the front of the craft, down the slope, and another two men held the tail. On the instructor's order, the team walked and then ran, stretching the rope. When he yelled 'los', the two men let go the tail and the glider was catapulted into the air. Being left-handed, but having to control the column with my right, I proved very clumsy on the controls and I earned the name of 'stunt pilot'. But I got the 'A' and then the 'B', which was three flights of more than one minute, with turns in both directions. It was clear to me, however, that my flying was more good luck than good control.

Near us was an experimental glider workshop led by a remarkable designer named Lippisch. His test pilot was a young glider pilot named Gunther Groenhoff, the national sail-planing champion, who held several long distance and height records. He was the first to gain a silver 'C' for a flight of 50 kilometres and over 1,500 metres above starting point. We became very good friends and he invited me to join his launching team for the international competitions. He was the favourite to win in his newly designed sailplane. His one real challenger was an Austrian, Rudolf Kronfeld, whom I met again as a squadron leader in the RAF during World War II.

When the competition began, flying was held up by unsuitable weather. We stood by from dawn until dark, ready at any moment to launch. One afternoon a heavy thunder storm, with dark, swirling clouds and flashes of lightning came rolling up the valley. Gunther decided to launch and disappeared into the storm. We stood by the recovery vehicle waiting for the message telling us where he had landed.

After some hours we were told that he had crashed in the valley below. Several of us ran down the mountainside and came to the place in the thick forest where we could see the sailplane and a parachute caught in the trees. We were told by woodsmen that Gunther was dead in his parachute, which had not had time to open properly. I was very shaken. It was the first time I had faced the death of an admired companion.

On Sunday I joined members of the launching team in a Catholic church. I did not follow much of the Latin service but my ears pricked up when the priest read a letter from the Bishop of Fulda inviting all Catholics to vote next Sunday for the Central Party in the General Elections. The priest then gave a passionate sermon on the penalties of defying the Church in this world and the next. I was interested to read in the local newspaper later that in the village all but one vote was cast for the Central Party. But at the flying school almost all the votes were for the National Socialist (Nazi) Party.

I asked the chief instructor if I might take the advanced course in soaring. He advised me to take some flying instruction at a powered flying school to learn feel and control properly and wrote a flowery letter of introduction. I presented this letter to the instructor of a small powered flying school near Marburg-an-der-Lahn, where I had a friend studying at the university who offered to share his lodgings with me. The letter misled the instructor into thinking that I was capable of piloting his Klemm trainer. Communication between us was complicated by my small amount of German and his total lack of English. I had only once flown in a powered aircraft - when I paid five shillings for a circuit of the airfield as a passenger in a Cobham's circus plane.

My instructor got up in front of me in the small Klemm, a low-wing monoplane with a 60 horse-power engine. He did not bother with a voice tube, but explained in sign language the engine switches, taps and other controls. Then he shouted *'Wenn Sie von Boden wegkommen fliegen gerade aus'* meaning 'When you leave the ground, fly straight ahead.' The only word I thought I understood was *'haus'*. Sure enough, after we had bounced across the strip with engine at full throttle and lifted above the trees, I saw a large white house ahead. So I turned the aircraft, applying full ailerons and rudder, as I was used to doing on a glider. The Klemm made to roll at this fierce control movement. The instructor seized the controls and moved them central. I had never been in a dual-controlled aircraft, so I assumed the wind was pushing the controls central, and pushed harder. The instructor turned and banged the windscreen in front of my nose and shouted '*los, los*'. The agony and fear in his face made me let go and hold up my hands.

He landed the Klemm, dashed into the clubhouse and came out clutching a tall glass of beer, which he gulped down. Then we had an excited conversation, with my little dictionary flashing back and forth. After that we flew with headphones on, having rehearsed the commands he was likely to give.

I learned enough at the school to return to the Wasserkuppe to take the advanced gliding course and win the 'C' licence - five minutes above starting point with properly executed turns, approach and landing. I believe I was the sixth Englishman to receive it, and probably the youngest. It was not achieved without one accident. I was soaring a Falke two hundred feet up when I went into a spin. I had no idea how to get out of a spin. The Falke made a couple of turns and hit the ground. It broke up into small pieces but fortunately the ground was wet and soft and I walked away, feeling sick but unhurt. Achieving the 'C' convinced me that I was going to get into aviation as a pilot.

While I was at Marburg I learned more than power flying. I got some insights into German life. The university student, Hans Stech, who had invited me to stay with him, initiated me into some student activities. He belonged to an ancient society, Germania. These societies, of which there were several at Marburg and in most universities, were centres of culture for their members' social life, fencing and drinking their main activities. Each wore a cap and band whose colours proclaimed their membership. On joining, each accepted a discipline of behaviour, dress and participation in the society's events, and severe punishment if one let the society down.

Hans took me to the Kneipes, the drinking sessions, and to the duelling. The fencing was a real test of courage. It was fought with sharp swords, and with a bare head and face. Blows had to be downwards or sideways and aimed at the head. The fighting involved cuts, blood, and pride in the courage they had shown. Regular fights were not matters of defending one's honour, but tests of manhood. On issues involving honour, heavier swords were used. I watched from a front row seat at an out-of-town inn, and asked if I might have a go, but was politely refused. I was told that these duels were prohibited by law, but winked at by the police. However, the students could not risk a complaint from me, had I been injured, as I undoubtedly would have been. I recall how impressed I was by the expertise of the medical students at sewing up faces. Of course, they had a lot of practice.

One of the drinking bouts to which Hans took me lasted for three days and nights. Another that sticks in my memory was held in a brewery. It was 'on the house', and we hit the beer hard. At some point in the evening I and some of my companions became bored with the singing and noise and went down the village street to another pub and poured down the Schnapps. Back in the street I collapsed, helplessly drunk, but conscious of the villagers gathering around me, laughing, as I lay in the road. I awoke in bed in my lodgings with the all-time headache of my life.

That summer of 1931 in Marburg many of the students
were being enrolled in the Sturm Abteilung Hitler
legions. Hans was among them and he took me along
to the parades - hundreds of marching youth in their
brown shirts and swastika armbands, singing through
the streets. I could see the Nazis were going places
and capturing the youth with big aims and demanding
discipline and sacrifices. I was impressed, as most
youngsters of seventeen would be, in that atmosphere
where you did not think, you followed. At that time
in England there was little get up and go spirit, and
young people like me yearned for it. In both Germany
and Britain at that time there were growing unemployment and hopelessness, while politicians
manoeuvred and denounced and looked out for their
own interests.

There were at least thirty political parties in Germany that year and I went to some of their parades.
The most impressive and frequent were the National
Socialist (Nazi) parades, with hundreds of students in
their brown shirts and breeches moving with discipline. The Nazi challenge was along the lines of an
appeal to sacrifice and patriotism. Nazi posters proclaimed: 'The German youth does not smoke', and
'The German girl does not make up her face'. I saw
little evidence of the evil thing Nazism was to become.
One incident which I put down at the time to student
high spirits happened at a lecture I attended at which
a Jewish professor was shouted down and driven out
of the hall with blows.

The following year, 1932, I returned to Germany to take an advanced gliding course near Kassel. I found a number of German soldiers enrolled in the course. I got on well with them, and they with me, and was invited into their barracks and saw the 'not permitted' tanks and other military equipment that they manned. I still did not realise the significance of their involvement in the gliding as a means of bypassing the ban on military flight training, as Germany began its building of an air force. Nine years later, as I flew over Germany at night on bombing raids, I wondered if the German fighter pilots hunting me might be the same men with whom I learned to fly in Kassel. I comforted myself with the thought that those men had probably by now been promoted to Generals.

I returned to Germany twice more before war closed the frontiers. As I travelled, my German had improved sufficiently for me to be taken as a German, though they detected something different from my accent. Germans from the south would ask me, 'Aren't you from Hamburg?' or, in northern tones, 'Aren't you from the Black Forest?' Yet I could barely write a word and I had no grammar.

In 1935 I had an added incentive to visit the country. While ice skating at my uncle Leo's rink, I had met a delightful girl from the Harz Mountains in middle Germany named Renate. She was a blonde beauty and I became very fond of her, and she of me. I went to her home and met her family. Nearby an air force flying school had been opened, and I heard that they had lost eighteen pupils in flying accidents in the

previous weeks. I thought they must have been working under a great deal of pressure.

One day Renate took me for a walk in the woods.
She suddenly stopped, told me to stand still and went
and looked around behind all the trees. Then she sat
down and to my surprise, for I was expecting something different, began to whisper about a terrible place
near there which she called a 'concentration camp'.
Clearly it distressed and frightened her, but its horror
did not impinge on my mind.

I was equally obtuse when I was travelling through
the country and stayed the night in Bremen in the
home of a young woman I had met. The family was
Jewish and well-to-do. In the late evening we heard
marching feet in the street below the flat, stamping,
singing and shouting. The family were clearly mortally
afraid and told me it was the S.S. (Hitler Bodyguard
men). Then came terrifying sounds, glass smashing,
the crash of doors being broken down, cries, shrieks
and drunken oaths. I wanted to look out of the
window, but the family begged me not to or make any
sign that the flat was occupied. I had never seen
people in such terror, but I didn't draw any conclu-
sions from the incident, certainly not that such scenes
would be allowed to grow in Germany and other
countries until war became inevitable.

Back in Britain, I learnt that a College of Aeronautical
Engineering was to open in Chelsea, in London. I
immediately put my name down for the first course.
Mother paid for the first term for me to train as an
aeronautical engineer. I soon found that there were

two types of students in our classes; a few like me who were out to learn all we could and worked hard, and the many who aimed to do the minimum and spent a lot of their time gossiping around the stoves and work benches, mostly about girls. One day one of the instructors said to the few of us, 'I don't know why you fellows pay out all this money to be taught this stuff, when you can learn it all in the Air Force and be paid to do it.' As soon as I got off work I went around to the RAF Recruiting Office and asked for particulars.

I applied for a short service commission of six years as a pilot, with a further four years on the reserve. I had no idea what competition I was running into for how few places. When I got to the interview and medical examination I found dozens of fellows, most of them the dead spit of me. But from this crowd two of us were selected. I wondered, why me? Perhaps it was because my colleague and I stood out as a result of having done something unusual. I had trained as a sailor and gone gliding in Germany, and the other chap had been flying light aircraft around northern Canada, summer and winter. The RAF taught us to fly all over again, but first we had to wait nine months before the Service took us for training.

2

Pilot Boy RAF

In September 1932 I reported to the RAF Depot in Uxbridge, near London, as an Acting Pilot Officer to start my six years service. There were twenty-five of us between the ages of eighteen and twenty-three. I believe I was the youngest, but because of my naval drill at Pangbourne it was easier for me than it was for the others. We did our 'square-bashing' (drill), learnt whom and how to salute and pay compliments to, and all the other rudimentary officer-like virtues. I was tremendously impressed by the drill sergeants and warrant officers who led us through the course. They had the skill and the ability to put the fear of God into officers while never once stepping out of their place as non-commissioned officers.

After a month we were moved to Lincolnshire No. 3 Flying Training School at Grantham. I well remember the fine figure of the Commanding Officer, Group Captain Richard Peck, in his No.1 dress - knee-high black riding boots, blue riding breeches and medal-be-ribboned tunic - sitting on the front of a desk as he addressed us. 'You have come here to toil,' he said, 'and toil you will.' We were worked hard, but no

harder than at Pangbourne, which I had enjoyed. And
as a matter of fact we had a marvellous time, with
flying, sports, mess life and good comradeship. Our
one big complaint was our No.1 dress - boots, puttees
and riding breeches. Not only were puttees difficult
to wind on your legs so that they looked even and
neat but if you had to pilot they were tight and
restrictive. A year later the RAF gave up this cavalry
uniform.

On our second day our flying instructors took us
up to show us the district and what an aircraft in flight
felt like. Most of the pupils had never flown before.
At supper that evening we noticed that one of our
number was missing. No one seemed to know why,
until rumours of his death were confirmed. Both he
and his instructor had been killed in a low-flying crash.
I don't remember anything appearing in the newspapers, although an RAF crash was rare and usually
front-page news. But I may have missed it - I was not
much of a reader. I was interested that the deaths did
not fash me, nor seemed to trouble the other pupils.
Maybe that was because we had not really come to
know each other, or were too self-concerned and busy
learning how to stay alive.

I was one of a group who found ourselves pioneers.
I was assigned for *ab initio* training to a Flight newly
equipped with De Havilland Tiger Moths. Until recently initial training had been done on a World War
I aircraft, the Avro 504. Now our school was giving
service trials to two new trainers, the Tiger Moth and
the Avro Tutor, a bigger and more expensive aircraft.
In the event, the Tiger Moth won the day and became

the world-wide training plane for and throughout World War II. We were also the first guinea pigs to be tried out in a new training technique. From the first day we were taught to fly by reference to instruments in the cockpit, instead of by 'the feel of the seat of our pants,' the rule until then.

I much enjoyed everything - piloting and handling controls, map reading and elementary navigation, though I was always a bit scared of the flying, and particularly of getting lost over Lincolnshire, which is flat country with big square fields and few landmarks. In autumn and winter visibility was often indifferent, with much cloud and sometimes strong winds. The one feature near the airfield which helped me was a Roman road, running north and south, a line ruled across the countryside. Like all the rest, I got lost around the airfield from time to time, but an east or west steering cut the road, and then up or down or both, until the airfield appeared.

After six months we graduated to heavier service aircraft. Those who were considered most suited to fighter aircraft went to the Flight equipped with Siskins, elderly biplanes of metal and fabric. The rest of us went to the Armstrong Whitworth Atlas, a two-man biplane originally designed for co-operation with the Army and as a light bomber. I was not sorry to miss the Siskin. It had the reputation of responding to an error in landing by turning on its back, banging the pilot's face against the instrument panel which could give you what we called 'the Siskin nose'. One day I watched a pupil in a Siskin take off and then hit the slip stream from another aircraft. The Siskin went into a roll and dived into the roof of the maintenance hangar which was filled with aircraft under overhaul. Fire broke out and soon there was nothing left of hangar or aircraft. Two men in the shed saw the pilot, one of our pupils, fall out of his seat on to the floor. They ran to him under the fire and pulled him out of the building, almost unhurt.

It was impressed on us that, while the Atlas was a safe aircraft to fly, it must not be put into a spin since, in certain circumstances, it would develop a flat spin from which it was very difficult to recover. So I was very careful never to fly the Atlas at the stall in a way that a spin might develop. One day a new instructor took me up on a height test, and for the first time I climbed the Atlas to 10,000 feet. Suddenly he said, 'Let's see how the Atlas spins,' and took over the controls. He stalled and kicked on full rudder. Down went the nose and round went the earth below. After three revolutions he moved the controls to correct the spin - stick forward and opposite rudder. The revolutions continued. I suddenly began to wonder how I would get out to use my parachute, where to grip and where to put my feet. Then the rudder kicked and the engine burst into a roar and slowly the revolutions decreased and we finally came out of the dive at about 2,000 feet. The instructor said nothing throughout, nor mentioned the experience afterwards. I suspected he had never tried to spin an Atlas before, and never would again.

When you fly, you are always at the mercy of carelessness - yours or someone else's. One summer day, with white cumulus clouds around, I was sent up in the Atlas to practise aerobatics, particularly the roll off the top of a loop, known as the Immelman turn. I climbed upwind of the airfield to about 5,000 feet and chose a fine clump of cloud into which I dived, then pulled the stick back until I was inverted just above the cloud. Then, using the cloud top like a table to judge my level and accuracy, I rolled off to the upright position. After making four rolls, as I levelled out above the cloud I opened up the throttle, but the engine did not respond. I quickly put the Atlas into a glide and steered away from the cloud towards the airfield, downwind of me. I checked the petrol taps, the switches, and tried opening the throttle. No response from the engine. I looked down at those big Lincolnshire fields and they seemed to shrink. I said to myself, 'I'll never get her down in one of those.' I sweated. Finally, I managed to set her down in one corner of the airfield.

I waited. After a while, the Hucks starter arrived, mounted on its Model T Ford. I could almost hear its crew, disturbed from their reveries, muttering, 'another d—d pupil has stopped his engine on landing.' They engaged the driving rod of the starter to the propellor hub. Then the driver shouted, 'turn off your petrol.' Petrol was gushing out of the bottom of the engine because the main filter had fallen out.

Later I found out that a mechanic servicing the Atlas had just screwed the filter in finger tight when the tea van arrived and he ran to be at the front of the queue. Afterwards he forgot he hadn't finished the job by tightening and copper wiring the locking ring, but signed the inspection sheet that the job was done. His sergeant counter-signed without verifying, which cost him his stripes. Most of my fellow pupils seemed ready to take up aircraft in blind faith that maintenance had been done satisfactorily. From that date on I made my own checks. I also started taking an interest in the airmen doing these responsible jobs, and thereby learnt a lot from them.

Early in my flying days I decided that my career lay in civil aviation and I wanted to prepare myself both as a pilot and a ground engineer. For this reason I asked to go into the heavy bomber side of the RAF, but as so often happens in the military, the authorities had other ideas. I was posted from Grantham to a light bomber squadron in Norfolk. However, I found another pupil who had been been posted to heavy bombers and who did not want to go. The school allowed us to swap places and I went to 99 Squadron at Upper Heyford, north of Oxford. I learned later that my colleague, after a few months in Norfolk, was sent to armoured cars in Iraq, where he stayed for four years - not much flying in that.

When I reported to Upper Heyford I found my squadron was equipped with the Handley Page Hinaidi, a very ancient aircraft developed from the World War I HP 500, used to bomb Germany. It was a very large biplane with two engines, a huge tail - which made it very difficult to taxi across the wind - and an enormous tailskid. Instead of the usual three-way control column, it had a big wheel and a fore and aft bar. Response to the controls was so slow you feared they were not working, and so you tended to over-correct.

Soon after we new boys started flying solo on the Hinaidi we were sent to an armament practice camp in Yorkshire. We were given the job of flying around the ground targets, for the front and rear gunners to fire at them. It was windy and very wet and we had to fly these wallowing old aircraft at about 150 feet, up and down and turn around madly whirling the control wheel left and then right, trying to keep her in a turn without falling into the water or entering the clouds. By the end of a 45-minute sortie I was bathed in sweat inside my bulky flying suit and my hands were tired and strained. On most other flights the captain was piloting, while I crouched beside him with maps and the chart board, trying to keep track of where we were and when we would reach the next turning point.

Not all the perils I faced were in the air. In November 1933, I was ordered to attend a church parade one Sunday. I had already arranged with my girl friend, Eileen, to have supper and go to a theatre in London. I drove my little Austin up to town, had a happy evening, then set out to drive back to Upper Heyford, still dressed in white tie and tails. At about 3 a.m. and a dozen miles from Heyford, close to RAF Bicester, my car went into a skid, rolled right over and on to its wheels again, while I was projected through its canvas roof, to land beside the road unconscious. I must have recovered consciousness quickly, because I was not yet cold, though everything around me was covered in ice. As I moved to get up I hit against a

milestone. A few inches more might have seen the end
of my days. As I look back I suspect it must have been
black ice that I hit; at the time I had never heard of
such a thing. I could not make the car start, so I walked
the mile or two to the RAF Bicester and persuaded the
gate guard to telephone Heyford and ask for transport
to fetch me. It was about 5 am when I staggered into
my room and lay on my bed feeling dreadful, but
determined to be on parade at 9 a.m. My batman came
in with tea and looked horrified at what he saw. He
hurried out to call the doctor. The doctor came and
said he must move me into the Station sick quarters.
I was adamant I was going on parade, which made
him suspect concussion. The doctor was persuasive
and equally adamant. I was feeling more ill by the
moment so I decided to undress. It was only then that
I realised how bloody and dirty I was.

It was not long before I was in an ambulance, being
driven 25 miles to the RAF hospital at Halton, Bucks.
I stopped the ambulance as we passed my little Austin,
looking crushed beside the road, and waved it a last
farewell. I was admitted for abrasions, cuts and suspected concussion. I found I was the only bed patient
in this officers' ward, though there were a few 'bed
and breakfast' patients who returned in the evenings.
It took a week for my cuts and bruises to heal and
then I felt aggrieved that I had to remain in bed, use
bed pans, and be bathed by nurses. When an inspecting doctor came round I remonstrated. His reply: 'You
are in here for concussion, and that means a month in
bed. If you continue to complain I shall treat you as a
real concussion patient and keep you flat on your back

in a darkened room. You count your blessings.'

From the hospital, after a short leave, I was sent to the RAF Depot at Uxbridge, outside London, and was put to work superintending the airmen joining the service before going for training in the different trades. I learned a lot about drill, supervision, inspecting barracks and how to mould men into good airmen. Again, I was impressed by the quality of the non-commissioned officers whose primary job was disciplining these men and convincing them about the service way of life. This also helped me to be much more understanding of the men and the difficulties they had learning to live in crowded quarters.

Early in 1934 I was posted to a famous old bomber squadron, No.7, at Worthy Down, near Winchester, Hampshire. Theirs was a fine station on a windy hill top. The squadron was equipped with another big biplane with a 90-foot span, the Vickers Virginia. It had a forest of struts and wires, a fuselage of aluminium tubes covered in canvas, two Rolls Royce water-cooled engines, a monocoque forward section holding four of the crew in open cockpits, and a gunner's position at the end of the tail, isolated from the rest of the crew. I seem to remember we became airborne at about 50 mph, climbed at 65, flew level at about 75, glided engines off at 85 (to keep control) and touched down at around 50. The longest flight I made in a Virginia was seven hours, but I believe it could stay up for nine on full tanks.

Our crew consisted of two pilots, captain and second, who also did the bomb-aiming and navigating, a wireless operator, a front gunner and a 'rear-end Charlie' gunner at the tail. We wore sidcot flying suits lined with wool, heavy flying boots, sometimes electrically heated, heavy gloves over light ones, leather helmets fitted with speaking tubes and heavy goggles protecting the upper part of the face, which was projecting out of the top of the cockpit.

Despite all this protection from the cold, in almost every flight I lost all feeling in my feet, often in my hands, and felt my face frozen. Meanwhile I tried to keep a written log of tracks, turns and headings, calculate wind speed and direction and the course to steer, while balancing a chart board on my knees, with its pencils and log book.

The truth was that navigation meant looking over the side to see railways, lakes or towns, or lights at night. It also meant depending on the long experience of our captains, who were mostly sergeants, to know where we were and not get too lost. One night, I recall, I wrote a wireless message to Worthy Down giving our position as 'twelve miles north of Bedford.' One hour later, my next message was 'fifteen miles south of Bedford.' We were flying into a 40-mile-an-hour head-wind.

Our Commanding Officer considered that his young officers would be better employed at tasks in the air that their so-called 'good education' had prepared them for, so it was navigating, bomb aiming and similar flying chores for us, rather than holding the controls and looking out over the side. Though we all kicked at the time, later on I was grateful for the knowledge I gained of general aviation, and also of

the problems the young aircrew experienced when
first they climbed aboard the aircraft.

Once my hotel background became known I was
elected Mess Secretary of the officers' mess, to run its
affairs and handle the caterer and staff. Later I was
responsible for the catering of the airmen's mess. I was
also put in charge of the station fire brigade, which
not only covered flying operations, but also fire
prevention and fire fighting of a town of some seven
hundred inhabitants, workshops, highly inflammable
stores and ordnance stores. Some married quarters in
my care were as much as three miles away. To this
day I am conscious of fire risks, barred windows,
escape doors and the working of fire extinguishers.

My CO sent me to a course at the Central Flying
School to learn to instruct in blind flying by instruments. On another occasion I took a course on the
operation of automatic pilots, with which the Virginia
was being equipped. In those days the young officer
could obtain a wide experience of management in the
RAF if he so chose. Most of us never guessed how
much we would need all this experience when war
came, with swift promotion, and many responsibilities
thrust upon us.

When the Wing Commander in charge of the
automatic pilot course at Boscombe Down learned that
I did not have an engineering degree or its RAF
equivalent, the big E course qualification, he forbade
me to enter the workshop. When I phoned my Commanding Officer, he was adamant that I was to take
the course. So I arranged with the Flight Sergeant who
did the instructing to post a look-out to give warning

of the Wing Commander's approach. Then I would take cover.

I found the auto-pilot a fascinating piece of machinery, new in design and with many challenging problems still to be solved. One of these major problems I had a part in solving. My squadron's aim was to win once again the Laurence Minot high level bombing trophy. Our CO realised that with the auto-pilot our bomb aimers could have a steadier platform from which to aim than could the manually controlled aircraft. So I was sent over to the Royal Experimental Establishment at Farnborough, Hants, to learn all I could about their experiments and to offer my help with the air-testing of new elements.

The auto-pilot was driven by air jets pumped in by an outside pump. However, whenever an aircraft entered wet air, such as a cloud, it might go into a roll or a dive or turn, or a combination of all three. The pilot had to release the auto-pilot rapidly from the controls and take over manual command because the auto-pilot malfunctioned. I found that this was caused by the rapid expansion of the wet air in the fairy valves of the auto-pilot, which caused ice to form and lock its valves.

I went back to Farnborough for aid and they produced a condenser which we attached to the side of the Virginia. It looked like the slide of a trombone. A quantity of silica gel was introduced into the condenser to dry the air. This took care of the problem and I was given the nick-name of Silica Gel Foss by those in the know. With this 'secret weapon' 7 Squadron again won the trophy - and incidentally was barred from subsequent competitions, supposedly to give others a chance.

While at Worthy Down I had other opportunities to test new equipment, largely because our station commander, Group Captain A.A.B. Thompson, who was an armament specialist, was also an enthusiastic inventor. He brought out several pieces of equipment for bomb dropping, and naturally our squadron conducted the trials. I was fortunate enough to carry out some of the tests, which added much interest to flying and bomb-aiming. I was also selected as an 'average pilot' for Farnborough trials. A few pilots were required to try out new equipment under service conditions after they had been passed by test pilots. I think we were chosen not only because we were about the average, but more so because we had the gift of the gab and could explain clearly why the equipment was not suitable or practicable, and to diagnose and recommend alterations. So many testers seemed unable to explain these things to the scientists, and just damned the item, which did not always help.

The squadron was re-equipped with Handley Page Heyfords, a bomber which cruised at about three times the speed of the Virginia, and was capable of operating at 16000 feet. We found a problem of extreme cold, specially in the open cockpit and even more when gunners had to stand up in the slipstream to handle their Vickers machine guns. So I was sent different types of flying suits, helmets, face masks and goggles to test. For one such test a flight was arranged for me to try out various clothing items for gunners operating the Scarff rotatable ring of the nose gun of the

Heyford. The station commander and other experts were in the cockpit to watch and measure.

At about 14000 feet I got up into the ring, where the temperature was minus 40F and the air speed around 160 mph. The pilot threw the aircraft about as though avoiding attacks, while I swung the gun from side to side, imitating firing it. I suddenly became faint and collapsed on the floor. I was pulled into the cockpit, the aircraft hurriedly descended and I was rushed to the doctor. I soon felt fine, but no one could explain why I had passed out. I was sent up to the Central Medical Board, who passed me out as 100% fit. None of us had realised that at 14,000 feet oxygen was in short supply and energetic operation of the ring and gun had caused me to be starved of oxygen, not helped by the severe cold and buffeting of the wind.

Further tests were called for to use the ring and gun without the face mask. Not one aircrew volunteered, so the doctor, who had become interested in these trials, volunteered himself. Up we went and at prescribed height he stood up in the ring, he claimed, for one minute. We in the cockpit timed him at fifteen seconds, when he had to be hauled back. His face, frostbitten, swelled to twice its normal size and developed black patches. We took photographs of it each day for a month until it came back to near normal.

During that year, 1935, the Heyfords took part in the Air Defence of Great Britain exercises, which ended the training year in July. We were instructed to fly out into the North Sea, towards Belgium and Holland, climb to 16,000 feet without oxygen, and fly into the London area. On the ground, at key military targets like the Ford motor works, which we were supposed to bomb, camera obscura were set up to plot our lights as we flew over and then mark the flash of our flash bulb which we signalled when we theoretically 'dropped our bombs'. From this could be calculated where the bombs would fall.

In the Heyford we had a beautiful and extremely expensive bomb-sight with which to aim when we picked out our target among the mass of lights below. In order to use the bomb-sight a window in the front had to be opened and the resulting blast of air was beyond human courage to withstand. So we gripped the bomb-sight between our knees, trying to keep it level, and sighted through the refracting glass window, to guess at the point to fire the flashbulb. We were never told, but I guess that not one of our Heyfords ever registered on the camera obscura screens, or even got within range of the targets. Oxygen-deprival could easily have made us believe we had fired, when in fact we had not, or seen a target when we had not. Lack of oxygen, unknown to us at the time, has that effect, but it does make you feel very confident.

On one of these raids a senior officer joined a crew. On his return he reported with horror that throughout the flight he saw the defending air gunners lying on the floor asleep. In his view, if they did not man their gun positions they should not receive aircrew pay, at that time, sixpence a day ($2^1/2$p). He seemed not to have realised that they failed to stand to their guns because it was humanly impossible without special clothing, face masks and equipment. It was his report that led to the testing of clothing and protection.

In those days the RAF totalled about 30,000 officers and men, about half in Britain and the rest overseas. For young officers like me it was a halcyon life, but it was very tough on the older men. In my Flight there were Flying Officers in their mid-thirties, many with combat experience, still awaiting promotion. They could scarcely live on their pay when single, married it was impossible. The CO's written permission was needed in order to marry. A marriage allowance and eligibility for married quarters, when one became available, were only obtainable by those over thirty. Those under thirty, married or not, had to 'live in' the mess - pay the mess dues and daily food allowance. My pay as a Pilot Officer was 62p a day and living in the mess cost around 30p. I managed to live on it, with Mother's help when I had to buy anything like clothing, and the tailor gave extended credit! At the same time, an officer was supposed to live the social life of a 'gentleman'.

Group Captain Thompson became troubled that around Worthy Down the local squires appeared to have little time for the 'ungentlemanly' RAF, who not only disturbed the summer evenings by their night flying, but were even rumoured not to dress in mess kit for dinner when ordered on night flying! Furthermore, when invitations had been received they had not been responded to. Locally the Army were the gentlemen, and since Portsmouth was near by, the Navy was acceptable. Thompson directed that all invitations must be accepted and he would personally select the officers who would represent the mess. We young officers were anything but enthusiastic, but we had no choice. Hitherto our idea of an evening's entertainment might be a pub-crawl around South-ampton or a visit to a music hall to raise a few boozy cheers and interruptions.

Out we went in twos and threes, selected and briefed by the Group Captain, to tennis parties, cock-tails and charitable events. One day we were sent to a Masque on a country house lawn. We had to dance a minuet with Mrs Thompson and local ladies cos-tumed in eighteenth-century clothes including full bottom wigs and swords. We had to attend rehearsals to learn the steps and, try though we might, there was no way to get out of the commitment. At the end of it all I was horrified to be presented with a bill for the hire of our costumes and also Mrs Thompson's cos-tume. We had dark discussions on how we might get *her* bill paid, but none of us dared to call at her house to see her about it. Finally, I resolved the problem by writing in the mess Bridge Book, which recorded winnings and losses at Bridge, settled monthly on our mess bills, that the Group Captain lost and I won the hire charge. It seemed that he did not carefully check his mess bill, for I heard no more about it.

The CO's social tactics did wonders in the area in those three years. RAF stock rose in local affections until it nearly equalled that of the Army and Navy, to judge by the number of marriages contracted with local ladies. Sadly, the Group Captain was killed a few days before World War II began. An aircraft landed with a live bomb hanging in its partially open bomb bay doors. The safety devices had come off. Thompson went underneath to inspect and try to defuse it. Someone in the aircraft misunderstood and opened the doors and the bomb fell on the ground. Thompson must have feared the fuse had been set off by the drop. He shouted to the crew above to abandon and he himself started to run - straight into the whirling propellor.

In 1935, when we were first beginning to equip with Heyfords, we thought for a time we might have to fly them into combat. Mussolini decided to invade Ethiopia, and the League of Nations ordered economic sanctions against Italy. It looked as though war might be let loose in the Mediterranean and the Middle East. 7 Squadron was alerted to prepare to go overseas, possibly to the Sudan. I was told to take the first Heyford to a packing depot in Cheshire to be measured for packing cases to freight it overseas by sea. The Depot CO asked me for the handbooks and technical books for the aircraft. I had to tell him that none had yet been prepared. No one seemed to have considered the possibility of shipping the aircraft to its theatre of war. Fortunately, a few days before, our Squadron CO had set his pilots an examination on the aircraft and its engines. I had done rather well in the test, so I felt confident to advise this CO how he might break the Heyford down into parts for shipping.

Nearly three months later, after much chivvying, word came that the Heyford could be collected. By that time the war scare was over and the crisis had passed. I went up to Chester to fly the aircraft back. The CO made it clear that my advice had not been much help, and they had had a lot of difficulties in taking it apart. I had some qualms about the air test of the re-assembled aircraft and its flight home.

It was just as well that the Heyfords were not sent overseas. The shortage of spares and equipment was chronic. I recall a line of us awaiting our turn to jump up and down on a motor car foot-pump to put pressure in the brake system after each flight; and the hours it took with this pump to blow up the huge six-foot high tyres. The Rolls Royce engines had no filters against dust and I suspect they would not have lasted more than a few hours in the desert conditions of the Sudan.

All in all, these experiences with the Heyfords were symbolic of the unpreparedness of Britain at that time to fight a war. My young colleagues and I in the RAF were not focussed on the reality of going into combat, and nor, I believe, was the country. More immediate for me at the time were my responsibilities as the airmen's mess catering officer. I was in the middle of a tremendous battle to lift the quality and service of the food. Grumbling about food became endemic and nothing I could do ever seemed to satisfy. I first tried putting every grumbler on the committee which planned the meals. It did no good; they had a 'them' and 'us' attitude and felt no responsibility to put things right. Then I made a practice of seeing each meal served up and of sampling it in public view. The standard went up markedly, but the grumbles only stopped when I announced that anyone who made a complaint which in my view was frivolous would be put on a charge in front of the station commander. It was high-handed, but it worked. I did not get a complaint for a month.

Although Mussolini's invasion of Ethiopia did not involve Britain in war, the events of the next months continued to put pressure on the government to increase our military strength. German troops occupied the Rhineland between Germany and France; Italy defeated and annexed Ethiopia; Spain was enveloped in a bloody civil war and Hitler and Mussolini proclaimed their alliance in the Berlin-Rome Axis. Pressure grew to expand the RAF and we in 7 Squadron felt its effects.

In 1936 we were moved to one of the airfields under construction at Finningley, near Doncaster in South Yorkshire. When we arrived it was a sea of mud, with most buildings not yet completed. The area was industrial, with many coal mines and the atmosphere was murky, a great change from our lovely Worthy Down and its glorious countryside. But another sign of RAF expansion, the promise of re-equipment with Wellesley Bombers - new monoplanes - lifted our spirits, only to have them fall again as the delays of delivery stretched out into months.

3

Steep Turns

Shortly before we left Worthy Down to move to Finningley, I had an experience that profoundly altered my outlook on life and made its impact on my professional career. It overtook me from a very unlikely direction - my two brothers, Hannen and Denis. In my view I played the role of 'Father' in our family. I was not only the oldest, but also an officer in the RAF, which gave me the responsibility, I felt, to provide the direction and advice which they badly needed. Denis, my younger brother, I regarded as indisciplined and uncouth, a serious embarrassment to me when he joined me at Pangbourne Nautical College. In fact, I rarely spoke to him there. When he went to sea, I had hopes that the Merchant Navy would straighten him out.

Not so. In 1935, Denis fell down a cliff and injured his back, putting him in hospital. He came home to our hotel to recuperate. I was horrified to hear of his wild activities in Bournemouth, which were not, I felt, suitable behaviour for the brother of an officer and a gentleman. When I spoke to him sharply about them I got an unprintable reply.

One day Denis went with a friend to some high-minded meeting to break it up. Instead, he told me later, he went to the chairman of the meeting, a Cambridge University graduate, and asked for a serious talk with him. Whatever they talked about, it seemed to have a remarkable effect on Denis. He went so far as to tell Mother that he had been responsible for shortages in the hotel till and he promised to pay back the money. More surprising yet, he went out and found himself a job cleaning out brine vats in a nearby factory, the only work he could get.

Brother Hannen, too, had been a disappointment to me. He was very bright and capable, and I had hoped he would try for the Foreign Office, and told him so. Instead, he joined a dance band in Southampton; his nights became his daytime. Then he was intrigued by the change in Denis and had a heart-to-heart talk with him and some of Denis's new friends. Hannen, too, became a new man, and soon afterwards left the band for work as a newspaper photographer, for which he had a great talent. It was the start of a life-time career in photography, films, television and film production. When news reached me of my brothers' transformation, my comment was, 'Very good and very necessary, but I doubt that it will last.'

When I enquired further into these changes I learned that they had come about through the influence of people known as the Oxford Group. I knew nothing about it, but hastened to make it clear that what I suspected was an 'enthusiastic' religion was in no way suitable for an RAF officer. Besides, I was quite certain that I needed no change. It was clear that my brothers needed to change and so did much in the world. I was told, 'If you want to make the world different, start with yourself.'

I soon perceived that if I were to take seriously what this was all about, there would undoubtedly be a price to pay, in passing up the flesh pots, attitudes and interests that I considered essential to my life. I was clear that such a change was not for me, and as a result I became sharply critical of my brothers and went out of my way to make things difficult for them.

But I found I could not quite enjoy everything as I had before. I began to take a fresh look at some of my activities. I had a regular girl friend of three years standing, a fine girl whose parents were very good to me. More recently I had taken up with two other girls as well. I hoped they might be more ready to bow to my needs. Of course I did not tell the girls about each other. I also realised that I was drinking in competition with older men in the squadron and was getting taken over by it. I was in debt, not by a lot, but mounting. I had always said that when I got a thicker stripe on my arm I would get out of debt, but it was not happening. I had thought that this was the normal way of life for an officer and gentleman and had claimed I was happy living it.

Then a couple of disconcerting things happened. One of my brother officers came to my room one day and began to describe the muddle and the troubles he had got into, and he asked my advice. Whatever I said to him, it had the effect of his bringing along another officer who seemed to be having similar troubles. I can't imagine why I did it, but I suggested that they go and see my brothers at a conference of the Oxford Group which they were holding in one of the Oxford colleges. Both men went for a weekend and came back looking and sounding very different. They thanked me warmly for advising them to go to Oxford, and encouraged me to go! I answered them a little brusquely, but I was intrigued.

Shortly afterwards I had to go into hospital for an operation and went home to the hotel to recuperate. To my dismay I found that a conference of the Oxford Group was about to start in the hotel. I found various excuses for not attending meetings, but in the end was persuaded to look in. I sat at the back of a gathering of about a hundred. The only speaker I can now recall was a large, soldierly figure, who rose and began to talk about a subject that I had never previously considered - sin. His talk was informal, amusing, personal, but sensible. To my discomfort, I felt increasingly that he was talking about me. I went hot and cold all over and sank ever deeper into my large, comfortable armchair. It never crossed my mind that there might be others in the audience who were feeling as I did.

At the end of the meeting I jumped up, dodged two men who looked as if they were coming to speak to me, dashed out to my little car and drove off to my RAF station. I had reminded myself that I was the Mess Secretary and that in two days we were to have a big dance there. I suddenly felt that I was essential to the preparations. Until that moment I had felt no responsibility for the dance, certainly not to cut short my sick leave. I worked hard helping put up decorations. I phoned a girl acquaintance to invite her to the dance, promising to drive her home afterwards.

I kept myself busy, yet I could not get out of my mind the ideas which the speaker had propounded. He had talked of four measures against which to look at your life: honesty, purity, unselfishness and love - each of them absolute. He said these standards could never be achieved absolutely, but they were like pointers in the sky; they could show you where you had failed and what you needed to do to straighten up. He had talked about 'listening to God' and told how he did it each day. I said to myself, 'I don't believe in God, but I must prove to myself that this idea doesn't work.'

After the dance I drove the girl home and stayed the night with the family. I was restless with this God-will-speak idea and could not sleep. Early in the morning the house was quiet and I felt sober. I decided to make an experiment and prove to myself that the whole idea would not work with me. I took a piece of paper and a pencil and sat up in bed. I said to myself, 'God, if there is a God, you can talk to me.' My eyes wandered over the walls and ceiling. I looked at my toes and out of the window. No flash, no bang, no voice, nothing. 'There you are,' I said to myself, 'It doesn't work.' Then, as I said it, a thought slid into my mind. I wrote it down. Then came another thought, and another, until I had written down four different thoughts.

I took a look at what I had written and realised that they were not normal thoughts of mine. Furthermore, if I were to try acting on any one of them, I had neither the courage nor the capacity to carry them through. I felt about them rather as one would about those mythical official documents marked, SO SECRET: BURN BEFORE READING. I did just that, took my piece of paper and burned it in the fireplace. No one was going to see what I had written. I tried to convince myself that nothing had happened, but deep in my consciousness a voice kept saying, 'You are a coward.' I had long tried to prove to myself that I was not a coward; in fact I joined the RAF partly for that reason. For two days I pretended that nothing had happened, but that voice persisted.

Finally, I decided to compromise; I would carry out my first thought, which was to be honest with Mother about the affairs I had had, and other misdemeanours. I loved her, but whenever we talked we were liable to have a set-to. I considered she had a sharpness of tongue that could cut the skin off the end of my nose at three-foot range. To be honest with my mother was the equivalent of stepping out of an aircraft without a parachute - madness, and very dangerous. I decided, but could not believe that I would have the courage to do it.

I walked to Mother's room with my stomach bouncing like a football against the floor. When I had finished, there was a long silence. Then, in a tone of voice I had never heard her use before, she started to talk. 'There are things about your father and me that I think you ought to know.' She went on to talk about their life together, the separation of wartime, and how the marriage broke up. It was the first time I had ever heard her speak of Father.

As Mother talked, a luminous thought came to me, something like a flashing neon sign above her head: 'When your Mother says "harsh" things to you, "Your tie is crooked," or "You're drunk," (as a greeting when I came home one day,) she is really trying to say "I love you," but the message comes out twisted.' At that moment I decided that I would never again be hurt by a remark of Mother's, because I now knew what it was she was trying to say. And I never was.

The second thought I had written down was to be really honest with my regular girl friend - to ask her forgiveness for my using her and her family without any intention of matrimony, which she and her parents might well have anticipated from my approaches. I shied away from that encounter for three weeks. One day I was ordered to go to the Central Medical Board in London for a check-up. This had always taken a full day. I arranged to be back at Worthy Down by the evening and expected this would bar me from having to go to Putney to see her. After little more than an hour at the CMB, a clerk said to me 'We have finished with you. You can go now.' I walked around the Aldwych wrestling with myself before finally deciding to go to Putney. My girl friend opened the door and I blurted out, 'Hello, I've come to have a talk with you.' 'Good,' she replied, 'because I need to have a serious talk with you.' Cowardly, I said, 'You talk first.'

She told me she had suspected that I had grown cold on her, but she had wanted to hang on to me because she wanted her girl friends to know she had a boy friend in the RAF. She said she was very fond of me, but added, 'I'm sorry to have held on to you like that and you must be free to break it off, if that's what you want.' I wished the floor could open up and swallow me. 'But that is what I've come to talk to you about, to say I'm sorry to be demanding of you, without any honest intentions.' Her answer was, 'Well, I forgive you and I hope you'll forgive me.' During the next hour I learned more about her than in all our previous three years. We had ceased to bluff each other.

My third thought was to make an apology to a fellow officer, an Australian. I had treated him badly, but until that moment I considered he richly deserved all he got. In those days officers from the Common-wealth were few in the RAF. We British were all very insular and critical of their different ways of speaking and their cultures, and especially towards Australians whose dark blue uniforms made them more notice-able. This Australian had not mixed well with the mess. If he saw two officers talking together and looking at him he seemed to think they were criticizing him. Then he would stalk over and threaten to slog anyone who talked about him behind his back. I had organised a ribbing campaign to get officers pretending to talk about him with glances and sniggers. Life must have been quite hellish for him.

I wrote some six drafts of a letter of apology before mailing it. When I got back to the mess, the Australian had left, posted away. I heaved a sigh of relief at not having to face him. A few weeks later, we heard an unusual engine noise from an aircraft landing. We went out to see a bomber of a new type. As I walked round the front I looked up to see my Australian climbing out of the pilot's seat. My heart quailed. Then I saw a look cross his face as though he too was quailing. He climbed out, dropped his chute on the tarmac and looked at his boots. After a pause he suddenly said, 'Thanks for your letter. I think you should know that I'm living with my wife again.' I hadn't known he was married, nor that he was separated, nor that this might have been a big contributor to his touchiness. I felt deeply grateful that I had posted that letter.

My fourth thought had been to 'run up my colours' in the mess and with the airmen in the auto-pilot section with whom I was working - skilled tradesmen, instrument makers. I had thought of them as 'men', and of myself as somehow superior as an officer. So I had never had any personal conversation with any of them. It was an enormous step in faith for me to stand up in the mid-morning break and tell them of the new standards I would try to live by, and invite their help and co-operation to do it. They sat around listening, with their cups of tea. Then the Corporal said, 'Thank you, sir. We'll try and keep you up to it.'

Several days later, I was preparing a stores return with the Corporal. I heard myself say, 'We can fiddle that deficiency, Corporal.' There was a pause and then the Corporal said, 'What was it you were talking about last Wednesday, sir?' I swallowed. 'You are right, Corporal, and we'll have to do what's right, and you and I know what that is.' It cost me some shillings, but it created a new atmosphere in the section. Very soon I found myself having talks with airmen about family matters and personal affairs. I seemed to be of some help and was grateful for a developing sense of friendship with some excellent men whom hitherto I'd treated as part of the misty millions who revolved around me.

In the officers' mess no one at first seemed to notice any change in me. One evening an officer said to me, 'What'll you drink?' I replied, 'Thanks, but do you know, I haven't had a drink in all of ten days. If I can go that long without wanting it, I can go on for good.' He made no comment and ordered a soft drink. For years I had said to myself, 'I could give up drinking if I wanted to.' In my heart I knew I couldn't, certainly not in the company of brother officers with whom I went drinking heavily from time to time. I thought it a manly thing to do, yet deep down I felt ashamed of the times when I got totally inebriated.

As I thought more about drinking and what was happening to me I realised several things. If I wanted to help anyone who, like me, could not say no, then for me to suggest the possibility of cure required that I did not myself touch a drop. I also realised that losing the compulsion to drink had been without effort or strength of will. Seemingly, my values and the direction of my life had changed, and so besetting habits and attitudes had fallen away. Could it be that there was indeed a force which was shaping and changing things for me? And could this force be God?

In the mess there was an officer I considered an intellectual snob. He came into the mess ante-room one day and in front of several officers made a biting remark about 'your religion'. I was at a loss how to reply, but at once two fellow officers rose from their deep chairs and walked over to him. One said, 'We don't like you. Foss is entitled to his ideas, even if we don't agree with them.' The other added in the fiercest tones, 'Shut up and leave him alone or you'll have to reckon with us.' I heard nothing further from this gentleman, and there came a time when we became good friends.

One man whose reactions I had greatly feared was my Captain of aircraft. He was a real beer and brawn man. After my return from my convalescence he took me up on local circuits and landings. As soon as we were airborne he seized the voice pipe and shouted, 'What's all this about you going off the beer?' I mumbled something and it was lost in the wind. As we touched down he made a big bounce and shouted, 'You don't think I'm going off the beer, do you?' I made a rude noise back. As we bounced into the air on the third aborted landing he shouted, 'Well, it will be a good thing to have one sober man in the car.'

My new-found change did more than alter my habits and relations with officers and men. I found a new confidence and concern about service matters. Soon after we arrived in Finningley I was sitting in the mess on a Saturday afternoon. Outside the visibility might have been a mile and a half and the cloud base a few hundred feet. It was very murky, and in those days not considered flying weather. Our fellow squadron was away in Northern Ireland for a practice camp, shooting, bombing and so on. A waiter called me to the phone, probably because I was the senior officer

Launch of a Zögling Glider on the Wasserkuppe Mountain in 1931.

Mrs Foss with her sons. Left to right: Denis, Merchant Navy, Patrick, RAF, and Hannen, Army.   *Positive Pictures*

A dual-control Sisken Fighter being started by a Hucks
starter mounted on a Model T Ford, 1932.

Handley-Page Heyford, 1935, — the last bi-plane bomber
to come into service with the RAF.   *RAF Museum, Hendon*

present. A police superintendent in Halifax, some forty miles away, informed me that an aircraft, which he believed to be one of ours, had crashed into the hills above the town and was burning. He believed the entire crew were dead.

I phoned the flying control Corporal and asked what he knew about an air movement; I already suspected it might be one of our Northern Ireland Heyfords. He knew nothing. I ordered him to open his control and summon the Duty Pilot. Then I looked through the Station Routine Orders to see who was the Station Duty Officer, who would be responsible in the absence of the Station Commander. It was our elderly Squadron Adjutant who lived off the station and had a problem with drink. As I feared, when I phoned him, he was not fit to take up duty. I said to him, 'Robert, listen to me. You are not the Duty Officer. I am the Duty Officer. You will find that Orders have been changed and you are NOT on duty.' He could not understand, but he did nothing. With the Orderly Clerk I created a revised set of Orders, naming me as the Station Duty Officer for that day. The clerk then went around the station substituting the new order sheet and destroying the old one.

Then I went to work. I phoned the wireless direction finding station (D/F), beyond the airfield, only to learn that it had been dismantled for a routine overhaul during the weekend. Phone calls began to flow in thick and fast. We heard the noise of aircraft engines above the cloud and the Duty Pilot began firing rockets, which guided the Heyford down through the murk on to the airfield. Its Captain told me he was part of a formation of seven Heyfords which had set out from Ireland. They had run into clouds and bad weather over northern Lancashire and had lost sight of their leader. This Sergeant had flown by dead reckoning until he glimpsed a patch of ground which he had identified and brought him near Finningley. The rockets had made it possible to land.

Another call told us that a Heyford had made a forced landing and finished standing on its nose; the crew were safe. A policeman in Lancashire had called to say that four men had landed by parachute; one of them had identified the sound of an aircraft overhead as possibly their empty Heyford, which would sooner or later crash. The policeman was calling for a county-wide alert. In the end, four Heyfords were destroyed and four lives lost. In the evening I drove to Halifax and up the hill to find the smouldering shell of the Heyford lying deep in snow. The Fire Brigade were removing the bodies. It was the first time I had seen a badly burned body or smelt the dreadful smell.

At the Court of Enquiry which followed I was an important witness. It never came to light that Orders had been changed. The Court's findings put much of the blame on a meteorological report handed out by an Ulster met. man. In my mind, however, I knew that the real blame lay with the officer who decided to lead the squadron back without notifying Finningley, ensuring that the direction finding station was working, or obtaining our local weather report. The men had a natural urge to get back to wives and sweethearts and their home comforts for the weekend. They had had an explosive farewell party with the Irish the previous evening, which surely blunted people's judgements.

At Finningley I was called on to undertake another new responsibility, the defence of an airman at a Court Martial. The man was accused of representing himself as an officer and of obtaining money by false pretences. It was usual for officers to defend men if they did not wish to have a solicitor. I had no previous experience and very little idea how to conduct a case. In the mess, before the case began, I heard the President of the Court say, 'This looks like an open and shut case. I hope we'll be through by tonight, because I've brought my fishing tackle and I mean to have a go at the North Yorkshire streams till the weekend.' It was not to be. The case ran three days and the President had to take down all the evidence in longhand because he'd not brought a shorthand writer. My client got three months. The press, local and national, made a meal of it when the juicy particulars came out. In order to do a better job defending men I learned some law and procedure, and over the next two years I was asked to defend several other clients, mostly on flying offences, and by chance got them all off.

In 1937, with about eighteen months of my short service still to go before transfer to the reserve, I was suddenly posted from Finningley south to Andover, Hampshire, not so far from my home. My posting was to 142 Squadron, equipped with Hawker Hinds and commanded by Squadron Leader E.C. de V. Lart. By this time I was a Flight Lieutenant. Andover was a very pleasant station, with two light bomber squad-

rons of Hawker Hinds and the RAF Staff College. I
never discovered why I, as an experienced heavy
bomber and night-flying pilot in a squadron about to
be equipped with Wellesley bombers, should suddenly
be moved to a type of squadron about whose work I
had no experience or ideas. Maybe some kind-hearted
personnel staff thought I would like to be near home
before I left my tour of duty, though I doubt that.
Maybe it was because my cousin, Peter Fidelis Foss, a
light bomber pilot, rather than I, was the intended
transfer and P.S. rather than P.F. Foss was posted.

Whatever the reason for my posting, it gave me
once again an interesting opportunity to learn another
aspect of the RAF. A few days after I arrived, some
distinguished foreign air force officers paid a visit. I
was sent up to lead a formation of nine to dive on the
airfield, simulating an attack. Up above six-tenths of
cloud, with eight fellows hanging on my wing tips, I
searched desperately for the airfield with its white
circle, our target. Suddenly I saw it through a gap
below us. We were flying in line abreast. I rolled,
kicked on rudder and was diving down on to the
circle. I pulled out around 1,000 feet and found my
whole formation lined up on me in Vic (Vee) formation. We looked very good. The visitors appeared
impressed.

Squadron Leader Lart, when he got me apart, said,
'Tell me, how did you get back into Vic like that, when
you started in line abreast?' I praised my pilots, who
had done their best with an inexperienced Flight
Commander. Shortly afterwards we were sent to
Belfast to fly a formation over the King in his Royal

Yacht approaching harbour. Then we were given the task at the RAF Display at Hendon of carrying out low bombing on a castle set up in the middle of the airfield, using practice bombs giving off white smoke. The crowds were huge, but the airfield was small. We had to take off from Hatfield because in rehearsal on take-off from Hendon two Hinds went into the crowd enclosure to avoid collision with a converging squadron.

Early in 1938 I flew up to Manchester to collect our first Fairey Battle bomber, a low wing monoplane with a Rolls Royce engine and a crew of three. Our flight up in the Hind took one hour and forty minutes. After I had learned the taps and other particulars, and had a circuit and landing, I took the Battle up, climbing above the broken cloud. There I tried the controls, changed pitch of the propeller, something I had not had experience of before, turned, flew slow and then fast, and by then had gained real confidence in the aircraft. After about fifteen minutes I looked over the side to see where we were. In the Hind we would have been about thirty miles down our return track. Nothing below looked right; I was lost. Then my experience in the Virginias, slowly ploughing across southern Britain, came to my mind. The soil colour below looked like the soil around Evesham. I suddenly realised that the Battle was flying at more than twice the speed of the Hind. We were indeed above Evesham. I was back in Andover in well under an hour.

My next task was to convert all our pilots on to the Battle, with a dual flying control fitted in the rear upper gunner's position, a spot totally blind ahead for landing, except for a panel I removed in the floor, through which I could see grass at the point of touch down. However, it was such a benign aircraft that all the pilots converted quickly.

The decision which had been taken to expand the RAF in a major way meant that in 1938 officers of any seniority or experience were being spread thinner and thinner as new aircrew and airmen flooded out of the training schools. Our opposite squadron, No.12 (The Dirty Dozen), lost its squadron leader and I was moved over, still a Flight Lieutenant, to take command. In this squadron the most senior officer was a newly appointed Flying Officer. All the others were new Pilot Officers and Sergeants.

In Europe the emergence of Hitler and the Third Reich was developing rapidly. After taking over the Rhineland, making a treaty with Mussolini, in 1938 Hitler annexed Austria. He kept his armies mobilised and threatened Czechoslovakia for its Sudetenland province. In September the British Prime Minister Chamberlain flew to Germany to persuade Hitler not to risk a war. He brought back his 'piece of paper' which in fact gave us twelve months to prepare.

It was in May 1938 when we were ordered hurriedly to disperse our Battles into the fields around the airfield in case our buildings were bombed. We cut gaps through the hedges and then came the rain. All our aircraft became bogged down and it took days to bring them back onto the airfield.

I called a meeting of the aircrews to consider how we would fight and defend the Battle. The gunners and wireless operators were all ground tradesmen who had volunteered to fly as aircrew, for which they received $2^1/2$p per day, as flying pay. As we discussed formations, cross-fire and high or low flying it became more and more obvious that the Battle was indefensible against a fighter attack pressed home. We were sitting ducks. A silence fell on the group. Then an air gunner asked a question that must have been in everyone's mind: 'Do you really think there's going to be a war, sir?' I replied, 'Well, it does look like that.' He said, 'I didn't join the air force to get killed.' A lot of the airmen agreed with him.

Eighteen months later these Battle squadrons were sent to stop the German tanks invading Belgium and Holland attacking bridges, railways and roads. They were decimated. The Battle was not heard of again as a fighting plane.

In July 1938 I was transferred to the reserve and I left the RAF. No one attempted to encourage me to remain despite the obvious shortage of experienced officers and pilots. For my part I felt that nations were on a path to war unless there was a profound change of spirit. It seemed to me that the Oxford Group and its programme of Moral Re-Armament was realistically trying to open eyes and minds to the one hope that could stop it. The day I left I dashed to Tilbury to join a ship leaving for Sweden with a party headed by Dr Frank Buchman. From Sweden we moved across Germany to Switzerland. On this expedition across Europe I met people, including Germans, who were striving to re-direct their nations' leaders from the courses which could only lead to a war. They were offering the alternative of seeking the wisdom and guiding of the voice of God.

This move into civilian life for a year was a rare privilege for a young RAF officer. The tour and subsequently working among dockers in the East End of London taught me about human nature, teamwork and courage. It was a unique preparation for the days of fighting and planning in the war years.

4

Amateurs at War

In August, 1939, I returned home to Bournemouth after finishing my annual training as an RAF reserve officer, during which I took a shortened flying instructor's course. I settled back running the milk bar I had started. One morning there was a letter in the post from Reserve Command advising me that in the event of mobilisation orders being issued I was to proceed to No. 3 Service Flying Training School at South Cerney, near Cirencester, Gloucestershire. My previous orders had been to report to a bomber squadron. I had no time to file the letter away when, barely three hours later, a telegram arrived ordering me to proceed in accordance with my mobilisation instructions.

I said goodbye to Mother, drew a week's wages from the bank for the milk bar staff and blithely assured the manageress, 'I'll be back in a week. There won't be a war. No one would be so mad as to start one. It'll all blow over.' Several customers and friends who were frightened came to ask my advice about buying extra provisions and the like. I reassured each of them. Most people were convinced that if it came to war there would be massive gas attacks and that civilians, despite the government's issue of gas masks, would die by the millions. We had no protection against the kind of gases the Germans might use on us, or we on them. Our fear about the threat of devastation by gas was very similar to today's reactions to the threat of nuclear weapons. In the event, neither side used gas.

I threw into my Austin Seven my uniform and items I might need for a week away and set off for Gloucestershire. On the road, I discovered that some authority had taken down most of the road signs. This was intended to confuse an invader. It certainly confused me and, I learned later, many others hurrying to their war stations or delivering needed stores and goods. Fortunately I had a good map. When I reached the vicinity of Cirencester I stopped to ask a farm worker who was trimming a hedge. 'Can you direct me to Sissister?' I was careful to pronounce the name the way I'd been told was correct. 'Where?' asked the local. I showed him the address on paper. 'Aah! You mean Zirenzester. It's over there,' he said, pointing the way.

A crowd of reserve officers and airmen was pouring into the station and I was directed to a queue awaiting a medical examination. I stood there, the last in line. The Medical Officer was patently unused to such pressure of work. By the time I reached him he was panting to get to the mess for a drink. He looked me up and down and said, 'You look a lot younger than the others.' I was twenty-five. 'How do you feel?' 'Oh, I feel fine.' 'OK, you're A1B,' he noted, grabbed his cap and shot off through the door. Just eleven months earlier, I had finished my service with the lowest medical category, fit only for limited flying duties within Britain. In less than two minutes, and without opening my shirt, I had achieved the highest flying category! It took the service about eighteen months to drop my category to about where it had been before.

I reported to the Chief Flying Instructor and found we had been together as cadets at the Nautical College, Pangbourne, and then again learning to fly at Grantham. He directed me to C Flight, one of two flights where pupils coming from primary flying training were checked and converted on to service aircraft and taught all the preliminaries of service flying.

As I walked along the line of huge hangars my morale sank and I felt lonely, out of my depth and really self-concerned. Then I came to a door marked C Flight, O/C Flight Lieutenant H. Kitson. With the entire RAF to choose from, here I was coming under the command of the man I knew best and most respected. As I threw up my salute to Hugh I felt that God had been very good to me to bring us together. Hugh seemed to be equally delighted to see me.

C Flight trained on a twin-engined monoplane, the Airspeed Oxford, newly introduced to the service. I found that most of the regular instructors at South Cerney despised the Oxford, much preferring the single-engined Hawker Hart, a biplane light to fly and very aerobatic. It gave an opportunity to display flying skills in a spectacular way. But in fact the Hart was out-of-date and the flying methods taught on it had largely to be unlearned before a pupil could be safe flying a high wing-loaded aircraft, such as the Oxford. The Oxford was not an easy aircraft to fly, but a pupil who became competent on it had little difficulty in converting to the big new bombers and other war aircraft now beginning to pour out of the factories.

The Oxford could display some frightening quirks in those early days of its development. If, by chance, and maybe not realising you had done it, you kicked the wing fillet (stream-lining) as you climbed up to get in, the Oxford, on reaching climbing speed, would develop a violent buffeting on the elevator control. This scared me the first time I experienced it, and it certainly scared pupils.

On 3 September 1939 war with Germany was declared. Our most urgent task was to train pupils to fly solo by night. I had spent four years in night bomber squadrons and had a lot of night flying time in my log book. When night flying was ordered, Hugh Kitson took me up in an Oxford and watched me make three take-offs and landings, then pronounced me ready to take up pupils. I was not so confident. Apart from the short flying instructor's course, I had done no flying for more than a year, and no night flying for more than two. In peacetime there had been lights everywhere below, but with the threat of war there was now a total blackout, not a light to help us see the ground nor to fly level. The one exception was the flare-path beside which we landed, a line of paraffin flares spaced over 650 yards, pointing into the wind. These flares were screened so that they were invisible above 2,000 feet and beyond three miles. There were a few hurricane lamps along taxi tracks, and one small electric light outside the door of the flying control tower. We all feared that we might lose sight of the flare-path and have no way of finding it again. We had no radio. Flying control was by an officer on No.1 flare with an Aldis flashlight with a green or red screen. In an emergency he could fire a rocket.

Most of our pupils came from RAF auxiliary squadrons, weekend fliers, mostly trained on Harts, but some were straight from Tiger Moths, the *ab initio* trainer. By the time I arrived, they had flown solo on the Oxford. C Flight was being doubled in size and additional instructors were joining every day. They were mostly from the Reserve, older and even less practised than I. Hugh Kitson had his work cut out to train these men to instruct on the Oxford. At the same time he had to build in new non-commissioned officers and maintenance airmen, and to expand the throughput of pupils to double what they had been handling. New orders demanded that flying be speeded up.

My first pupil climbed in beside me. He told me he had had one previous night's instruction. He taxied out to the first flare, where we got a green light to take off. I noted that we had passed the last flare before the Oxford lifted off and climbed into the pitch darkness. We made our circuit of the flares and signalled our light for permission to land. A green flash responded. We sank down towards No.1 flare and struck the ground heavily with a great bounce which I flattened with a burst of engines. Then we taxied around to prepare for the next take-off. We did our cockpit drill in our dimly lit cabin, got our take-off green and away we went again. This time around the pupil flew it into the ground without checking at all.

Once more I tried to explain to him how to see the
angle of the flares and ground and check the glide at
the right height for the Oxford to do a three-point
landing on wheels and tail.

Again we prepared to start and got the green. As
we raced down the flares the Oxford seemed to be
even slower in gathering speed and we had only just
got our tail up when we passed the last flare. I shouted
through the voice tube to the pupil to pull the Oxford
off the ground. The aircraft wallowed horribly as he
did so and began to climb very slowly. I saw the
boundary fence go by just below us. I called, 'Get your
undercart up' and noted his hand went down to the
levers between us. The Oxford began to sink down,
down. Our wing tip red light lit up branches of a tree
which flashed past. Our downward recognition light
illuminated a tiny patch of grass just below us. I seized
the controls and somehow clambered the Oxford up
to 800 feet before I handed back control to the pupil.

All the muscles in me seemed to be jumping and
inside my thick flying suit a cold sweat spread over
me. I felt sick. I took the voice pipe and said, 'By God,
you pulled up the flaps when you pulled up the
undercart. You must have taken the Oxford off with
the flaps right down.' The pupil replied, 'Oh, no, sir,
you would have noticed if I'd tried to take off with
the flaps right down.' Any practised instructor would
have noticed - but not me, on my first night flying and
my first pupil!

To land the Oxford the flaps are put right down,
both to slow the aircraft and increase the lift of the
wings. For the take-off the flaps are lowered to 30 per

cent, but shortly after climbing, when the speed has been raised enough, the flaps are lifted into the wing. The effect of raising the flaps from fully down, especially at slow speed, is to stall the aircraft so that it sinks until enough speed is reached to fly and then climb. What must have saved us from a crash, sliding along the ground at more than 100 mph, and surely our deaths or serious injury, was that in raising the two systems together, wheels and flaps, the hydraulic supply must have activated the wheel jacks first and only after that the flaps. The 'new boy' always seems to gather the emergencies, some he may not meet again for years.

That point was illustrated by another incident that same night. I had been trundling around the airfield all through the night with pupil after pupil. Dawn was near and I was pretty tired when my last pupil climbed in beside me. This pupil seemed unable to align the Oxford with the flare-path to make a landing. I had to send him around several times before he got sufficiently in line to attempt a landing. He banged the Oxford into the grass and bounced high diagonally over the line of flares. I took over control and opened up the engines wide to ease her on to the ground. As I did so a figure rose from near a flare and appeared to pass through the whirling arc of the propeller on my side. Once we were stopped I looked back and saw a prone body. My pupil became very distressed. I taxied fast to No.1 flare, shouted to the control officer and took the aircraft into Maintenance. Men ran up the flare-path to find an airman getting to his feet and holding his head. 'What hit me?' he asked. He had only cuts and bruises - a very lucky man. On the underside of the Oxford we found a score the depth of the wing and a flap split. In the exhaust manifold behind the propeller was a dent the size of a man's head. Why the propeller at full throttle had not hit him was a miracle. He was in that dangerous position to put out the flares in the unlikely event of a German attack without any warning.

Week after week, all through the autumn and early winter of 1939, we circled the airfield at night, training pupils. It was arduous and stress-making and we were not helped by the daylight duties we were expected to carry out. We all became very tired, errors began to creep in and accidents followed. One night a pupil and instructor lost sight of the flare-path and hunted about until they saw a row of dim lights. Just before they landed, they realised the lights were on a plat-form of a railway station. We instructors urged that the airfield be equipped with a flashing beacon, which could be turned off before a German attack. Finally, Authority relented and positioned a beacon three miles from the airfield. In January 1940, a heavy fall of snow closed the airfield and gave us a much needed respite. We instructors slept the clock around and the maintenance caught up with their arrears of servicing.

About this time the School had a visit from an inspector from the Central Flying School (CFS), where the long course flying instructors were trained. He was horrified to learn that persons like myself without a full CFS certificate were being allowed to teach pilots. We were moved to the advance training course, where we taught navigation in the air, formation flying, gunnery and bombing, while giving pupils much more flying practice in all kinds of weather. I found that advanced training demanded a higher degree of flying skill than my previous duties had required. If I was called on to demonstrate shooting from my front gun at a flying target, I had actually to hit the target in order to impress the pupil. Similar expertise was demanded with bombing or navigation.

At the School I had the opportunity to offer a more scientific method of assessing pupils' progress. Until that time the assessment of pupils had been left to the instructors, whose judgements could be highly subjective. As a result, pupils were being failed, after a lot of time and money had been spent on them. I offered the School a simple but comprehensive system: the pupil carried a card which both flying and ground instructors marked. The failure rate dropped, so that there were more pilots available a few months later, in July, when the Battle of Britain was fought, in which every available pilot was needed. Many of our pupils fought in this battle, which was a major factor in denying Hitler the possibility of invading Britain. A number of those pupils were killed or wounded in the air duels which were so costly to the German Luftwaffe and proved to be a turning point in the war.

In April 1940, the war on the Continent, which had been quiescent, suddenly sprang to life with the German invasion of Norway and Denmark. Then, in May, its true nature was revealed with the invasion of Belgium and Holland - the waves of parachutists, the emergence of fifth columnists, the heavy bombing of cities like Amsterdam without warning, the strafing by fighters of refugees on the roads. We in Britain had a glimpse of what we could expect from invasion. Urgent orders came to our station to prepare to defend ourselves.

The situation was not without its ludicrous side. Our Station Commander took it all very seriously, even though we were in the west of England. He was particularly concerned about a religious community, largely German-speaking, located about two miles from our airfield. He directed that at first light each day an aircraft was to be flown over the community to see if there were any parachutes lying about. His suspicions were heightened when the first reconnaissance reported that the whole community was up and about in the early dawn; he could not imagine anyone getting up at that hour unless they had criminal intent.

One day during that month of May, Hugh Kitson showed me an Air Ministry Order which invited volunteers to open a flying training school in New Zealand. He had volunteered and asked me if I would go with him to run the advanced training. Kitson was accepted. I heard nothing for several weeks. One day I went into the Chief Flying Instructor's office and looked through the papers on his desk. I found my application near the bottom of his IN tray. I placed it on the top of the pile. At that moment the CFI walked in and asked what I was doing. I pointed to my application. He said, 'It's not a bit of good your applying to leave here. You're much too useful to us.' I protested. He said, 'You know I am paying you a compliment.' A week or so later I was promoted to

Squadron Leader in the Reserve Officer list. So the CFI had to lose me, but not to New Zealand.

A couple of days after my promotion an urgent message arrived instructing me to move to Harwell, Berkshire, immediately. All clearance and handing over procedures were to be waived to speed me. I moved the same day and found an Operational Training Unit converting pilots and crews on to the Wellington Bomber before assigning them to squadrons. I reported to the Station Adjutant, who greeted me with, 'I'm afraid we've heard nothing about you. I suggest you report to the Link Trainer instructor, who'll give you some practice.' The Link Trainer was a simulator for blind flying on instruments.

That evening in the mess I met a Flight Commander and he asked me if I would help by acting as a safety pilot with the new pilots doing solo on the Wellington. Next day he gave me a few circuits on the Wellington Bomber. It seemed a lot easier to fly than the Oxford. Then, for the next week I sat up in the sky, day and night, watching new pilots flying solo on the aircraft. Suddenly there came a high level blast from Group Headquarters: 'Where is Foss? He is needed at once at No.115 Squadron at Marham in Norfolk.' Overnight I was taken off check pilot duties, found a crew who were completing their training, and made Captain with about four days of flying and training together. My log-book was certified that I had completed operational training and I was on my way to Marham.

Rumour had flown around that Wellingtons had been shot down by the score in daylight attacks over Germany. Long afterwards I learned that a few Wellingtons had been lost early in the war, when they were sent over Heligoland in broad daylight and without fighter escort to attack German naval vessels. After that, Wellingtons were used only at night. This rumour, together with my complete lack of training convinced me that we would all be killed in a few days. My apprehension was heightened just after arriving at Marham when I took a walk towards the airfield. As I approached the hangars there was a mighty explosion, with a great flash, and I saw much smoke and flames on the tarmac. In moments the fire engine screamed by, followed by an ambulance. Men ran here and there. Was it an enemy attack? No air raid alarm had been sounded. Later I found out that an airman, loading a photo flash bomb on to a Wellington, had accidentally triggered the fuse. He and the ground crew ran for it in the twenty or so seconds before the bomb exploded, and all were unhurt. It had blown the aircraft into small pieces and smashed a lot of windows.

I discovered that the urgent requirement for Foss's services at Marham was not as a replacement for casualties, but because one flight commander had been promoted and the other flight commander was due to go on leave. Without me to relieve them the war could have stopped!

5

Night Raids

In July, 1940, when I joined 115 Squadron, there were three RAF Groups operating night bombers, mainly against Germany.

The Wellingtons were in 3 Group, Whitleys in 4 Group, and Hampdens in 5 Group. Other Groups controlled the light bombers, fighters, coastal reconnaissance, and so on. All three Groups of night bombers had twin-engined aircraft with crews of between four and six. Bomber Command's attack plan called for raids each night, if weather allowed, on such 'military' targets as oil plants, factories, harbours and railway marshalling yards. When the moon was minimum one Group would fly each night. When there was a moon the three Groups doubled up, which meant we did a raid every other night. A raid was a major operation; a station complement of two thousand or more was needed to launch up to twenty Wellingtons on one night.

Aircrews lived a strange life. On our off days, on these comfortable, long-established stations, we lived like country gentlemen in a fair degree of luxury, and almost as if the war did not exist. On flying nights, we stole out like cat burglars to venture out, each aircraft singly, over the seas and into enemy territory, where we felt hunted and watched every minute. We flew in a high degree of tension. The sight of shells bursting in the sky ahead, often seen for an hour or more before we reached a target, had a mesmeric effect on me as my imagination leaped around. Highly subjective feelings kept me thinking more about my skin than about the people in the dark far below me. I did not want to die, nor have my courage tested by a shell burst or a fighter's attack.

I realised somehow I had to conquer this deep desire for self-preservation and treat the whole business as a surgeon would an operation. As each trip brought more near-misses by shells or close encounters with fighters, I became more and more conscious of the dangers, and I also began to question whether what we were doing was of any real use in the war. This helped me to understand why some men, their fear building up raid after raid, failed to press home attacks on their targets and instead dumped their bombs in the area before turning for home. It meant, of course, that they told lies to the debriefing officers, and their aircrew went along with them because they, too, were afraid.

It was the responsibility of a flight and squadron commander to know his men and understand the build-up of pressures, raid after raid. Each captain was different, and the commander had to judge when each crew should come off operations to allow them to rest and re-think, as well as to train new crews in all that they had experienced. At this time Command had set a tour of 31 trips. The average loss rate was around 25 trips, so every raid over 25 gave a crew the sense they were lucky to be still alive.

During World War I men were treated as cowards when they lost their nerve; and some authorities took the same line early in World War II. It proved to be a useless course; it encouraged no one to do better. The desirable way was to get a man to be honest and admit his fears and seek the support of his brother officers. When I did this with men, particularly when I became squadron commander in Malta, it seemed to have a profound effect on them, and on me too. I learned that the more afraid the average man is, the more likely he is to push home attacks and take risks, if only to prove he is not afraid. The bravest men, I found, were those who conquered their fear by facing it, not those who had no idea of the danger of what they did.

Looking back from the perspective of Malta on our time at Marham, I could see that we lived double lives - our 'gentlemen's lives' and our almost secret nefarious outings to Germany. In Malta our lives were all of a piece - we lived with the enemy over our heads, our quarters were bombed into rubble, our beloved photos and nicknacks smashed. We ducked in and out of caves; it was a very personal war. If we did not fight it, no one else would. Almost all of us experienced 'twitch', and other symptoms of stress in the eyes, the lips or the bowels. But the stress did not lead us to dump bombs or pull away from attack. It boosted morale in a remarkable way, so long as it was contained by a relationship with each other which was honest and caring.

Again, looking back at the raids we flew in the early days to attack 'military' targets, the marshalling yards and factories, I shudder at how amateur we were. The targets for new crews were the big railway yards at Hamm and Soest, on the edge of the Ruhr industrial area - Ham and Eggs was the obvious crew slang for them. They were large area targets and not so heavily defended as was the Ruhr area itself. There were planners who believed that bombing a railway yard would cause delays and disruption of communications. My own experience in 1938, before the war, of trial bombings of railway lines at the Army Corps of Transport railway experimental centre had convinced me - and the Army - that damage could be repaired in a few hours and did not cause much delay in a marshalling yard. These attacks were rather artificial, by low-flying Battles, but war experience confirmed that without continuous bombardment the yards were an unproductive target. However, our new crews did gain the experience of flying over Germany, of being shelled and hunted by fighters and of just how difficult it was to identify a military target from a great height in European weather.

My first bombing raid was on Gelsenkirchen in the Ruhr - the target was a factory. When we arrived in the target area thick smoke and layers of cloud made it impossible to identify anything as small as a factory. I was very suspicious of our visual navigation, although I had an excellent navigator and had myself been an experienced navigator in peacetime. Since we left England we had seen nothing to pinpoint our position. We could only release our bombs in the

general area and turn for home. The German reaction
with anti-aircraft flak and searchlights was strong and
accurate. As we flew towards Marham, some 300 miles,
our crew talked about the experience. Our conclusion
was that if that was the worst we would meet, we had
some chance of surviving our tour of operations. But
in my mind was the question whether we had bombed
the right town, let alone the specific factory.

On this and other raids our great problem was
finding and identifying a military target by our available means of navigation - map-reading, calculation
and hoping to find some identification near our target.
Our weather forecasters had only a general and
limited idea of the local conditions 300 miles from the
UK. They seemed unable to forecast smog or the
height of cloud layers.

On this first raid my navigator and I had hoped that
we might see the river Rhine and get a fix from that,
but we never saw the river. There was one aid on
which we came to rely heavily, the German range-type
wireless stations, which they switched on to aid their
own aircraft. We took bearings with our loop aerial.
But these only helped us to get into a four or five mile
area around the target. There came a night when we
filed into the briefing room before a raid and were
horrified to be told that no German radio station was
on the air. It would not have surprised me to learn
that each of our aircraft hit a different target that night.

On my next raid, to an oil processing plant at
Wesseling, near Cologne, we carried a photo flash
bomb with our other bombs so that we could photograph our target. My navigator and I worked out a

track to strike the Rhine at its junction with the Moselle. From there we would count the loops in the Rhine until we reached the one on which Wesseling lay. As we approached the Wesseling curve, my bomb aimer lay below me, looking down through the aiming window, directing me by inter-com, while the other four crew manned the fore and rear gun turrets and the look-out in the upper astrodome. The second pilot sat beside me, acting as counsellor, lookout and ready to take over the controls, should I be wounded.

In order to get a good photograph, the flash bomb had to be dropped at a precise height and the camera, fixed in the aircraft, had to be aimed so that the lens did not pick up the direct light of the flash, when the bomb burst after falling to about one thousand feet above the ground. The flash activated a photo cell which closed the camera shutter. This photography required that the Wellington be flown straight and level on a long run in. Straight and level at a precise height was a delight for German flak gunners!

This was another murky night, with a layer of cloud at the height we had planned to drop the flash bomb. We could see a Whitley bomber caught in the beams of searchlights, directly above our target, lit up by the reflection from the clouds as though in bright moonlight. Shells were bursting all round him. We decided to glide in below him, hoping the defences would not pick us up while they concentrated on the Whitley. We arrived over the target without being picked up and let go our bombs and the flash bomb. When the flash went off it seemed as though the defences were blinded for a few seconds. Then all hell was let loose at us. Shells began to burst around us; we could hear the explosions and see the black puffs of smoke. Our rear-gunner called that he thought he saw the lights of a fighter nearby. The searchlights bracketted us and I threw the Wellington into twists and turns to try to throw them off. They did not let go. Any moment could be our last. I sweated with fear as I pulled and twisted the controls. Then I offered up a prayer to be shown what to do.

At that moment an extraordinary impression came over me. I seemed to be outside the Wellington, away in the sky. I could see the aircraft in the lights and shell bursts, as though I were a spectator. Then I saw how I might break out of the defences if I made a highly dangerous manoeuvre. As I saw this, I had a feeling of confidence that what I should do was right. Then I was back in the Wellington, frightened and heaving at the controls. I pulled the aircraft up into a big stall turn, fell over and spiralled down towards the earth. Almost at once the lights shut off and we were falling in utter darkness. I eased the aircraft out of the dive to be parallel with the unseen ground. At that moment a single searchlight came on and laid along our track, showing us that we were a few hundred feet above the countryside, and lighting up hills ahead of us. The light went out and we climbed to avoid the hills and return to operating height for the flight home.

Back in the interrogation room at Marham we commented, rather smugly, 'The Commander-in-Chief calls our bombing "gardening" but wait till you see our photo of the target.' Air Marshal Sir Charles Portal, Chief of Bomber Command, had been invited by our

Station Commander to witness a demonstration of dive bombing by a Wellington. Afterwards the C-in-C talked to us about the pin-pointing of targets by night. He said we were digging up the German countryside with our bombs. He called it 'gardening.' It was not until 1942, with the introduction of the pathfinder force, who used radar to fix their positions and marked them with fires, that the main force bombers could be sure where the area of the target of the night lay.

A few minutes after our smug remark about gardening, the print of our flash photo was shown to us. It revealed a factory in a curve of the Rhine with four bombs bursting on the roof. Unfortunately, when we compared the photo with our detailed map of the target it in no way fitted. Someone suggested that perhaps the map was wrong. Wearily, we trailed off to bed. Three weeks later a report arrived from the Photo Interpretation Unit. They had identified the place where our bombs had fallen - a tank factory in Cologne, some ten miles from our intended target!

When the Luftwaffe made their bombing attacks on London in July 1940, the Prime Minister ordered us to attack Berlin. This was the longest trip we had ever attempted in the Wellington, close to our maximum range with full tanks and minimum bomb load.

We set off for Berlin with half a gale blowing from the west, low and middle cloud, and murk on the ground. We were given strict instructions to turn back after three and three-quarter hours flying, wherever we were, to be sure of returning to Britain against the gale. As I reached three and three-quarter hours we thought we might be in the Berlin area. We had failed to get any fixes on the route and the weather was heavy cloud and total blackness. We glimpsed below us lakes and forests, but never a light or other indication of a city. There was nothing worth bombing and no time for a search. We turned for home and began to plug back against the gale.

After an hour or so we saw lights on the ground, which we identified as an airfield working night fighters. We made to bomb them but our bomb releases failed to work. We plugged on and finally, over the North Sea, succeeded in losing our bomb load, saving us some petrol. We landed at Marham with less than thirty minutes of fuel remaining after eight and a half hours in the air. Our other crews returned with similar stories. No one was sure he had hit Berlin. We hoped other stations had had more luck.

A few days later, we were ordered to bomb the Channel ports, Calais and Le Havre, our shortest trips ever. They were on brilliant moonlit nights and we could clearly see the lines of barges waiting to carry the German army to invade Britain. From 6,000 feet they looked like match sticks. We had filled every hook with high explosives and fire bombs. The Germans had only deployed light flak guns, and these were less accurate at our height. I saw fires break out along the docksides and in the barges, followed by many explosions. On one raid I saw quite clearly water jets being played by firefighters - the first time we had seen a result of our attacks. Thanks to the efforts of our fighters, the Germans never achieved the air supremacy over southern England which they needed for a successful invasion. However, the destruction wrought by our bombers on the ports and barges must also have played a part in their decision to call off the invasion. That decision ultimately meant losing the war.

In August 1940, we made a long trip towards Magdeburg to attack an aircraft factory at Bernberg. The night was clear and moonlit and I could see the Hartz Mountains where I had visited friends in 1932. We passed near Goslar, the home of my pre-war girl friend. When we reached our estimated time of arrival we were delighted to see below us a cross of big runways and sheds, but I was not sure that this was our target so put the second pilot in my seat and went down to lie beside the bomb aimer to have a better look. I had been troubled by seeing, some five miles to the south, bombs bursting and flak coming up and wondered if that was the right target. As we lay there, trying to decide, suddenly our Wellington went into a steep dive and then we saw our bombs leave and crash through the roofs of the sheds. As we pulled out of the dive, chunks of the roofs flew past us, very close. At once guns opened fire and I could feel strikes on our aircraft. At the same time a force, like a giant hand, seized our Wellington and threw it upwards. Once we were away from the target area the second pilot started making excuses for the attack, saying we were running out of time and he was sure that we had found the right target.

I went all around the aircraft to see what damage we had sustained and found nothing that was serious. However, I was very troubled that each of our three compasses seemed to be giving a different reading. We attempted to verify them by the moon, but without moon tables or a sextant we failed. So we averaged the three readings and steered a general westerly direction. Clouds now prevented us from fixing a position. When we expected to reach the coast we saw a coastline and a flashing beacon. In a discussion with the crew, one of them thought the beacon might be on the English coast, so we flew close and fired our recognition signal, a verey light giving the colours of the day. It was answered by light flak and we dashed out to sea. In a couple of minutes we passed over a bund and then wave crests. This convinced me we must have crossed a part of the Dutch Zuider Zee, and if so we were embarking on a flight of about 150 miles across the North Sea.

I checked our fuel gauges and found several were showing nil and others only small amounts of fuel, maybe half an hour's running, certainly not enough to get us beyond the middle of the North Sea. We seemed bound for an emergency landing at sea, something none of us had rehearsed; indeed, I had no idea even how to activate the dinghies. I doubted whether air/sea rescue boats operated so far out. I asked the crew for their suggestions. One option was to turn back and land on the beach and surrender ourselves. No one would hear of that. So we continued westwards. As we strained our eyes looking for land, we kept seeing it, only to find it was cloud on the water.

When I asked the wireless operator to try and get a bearing from the Direction Finding service in England, he told me his wireless was playing up, but he would try. Then he told me he could hear several S.O.S. calls, and that meant that the D/F stations would concentrate on them. I insisted he keep trying and he finally received a bearing. I plotted it on the chart; it was almost due north and put us out in the English Channel.

I couldn't believe it. I asked our operator if the bearing could be a false one put out by a German station. They were known to give false bearings to our aircraft in distress. If we were half way across the North Sea and turned north we would go down in the cold sea en route to Iceland. The operator assured me it was a good bearing from an English station. I swallowed my doubts and turned north. The sun was up, but cloud was solid below us. Suddenly there was a gap and I saw a green field. I pulled back the engines and dived for this break. I saw fields dotted with high posts and other anti-invasion obstructions; it must be the south of England. I gingerly opened up our engines again, noting that every fuel gauge registered empty.

Suddenly, right ahead, appeared a grass airfield, apparently empty. I dared not circle to look more closely because if we banked our wings the petrol might run away from the outlets and stop the engines. I shut down and went straight in. As we ran across the field I noted large piles of earth dotted about. We came to a halt beside a flying control building with no sign of life. We got out and began to look for someone. We came upon a sandbagged shelter and out of it peered a steel-helmeted RAF figure, a Pilot Officer.

Hawker Hinds of 142 Squadron rehearsing for Hendon Air Display in 1937, led by the author.

Vickers Wellington IC, 1940. *RAF Museum, Hendon*

Preparing to fly to Africa on 1 January 1947 in a Percival Proctor III. Left to right: Andrew Strang, the author and Charles Burns.

Lieut-Colonel Alan Knight, Commandant of the Athi River Detention Camp in Kenya, with Nahashon Ngare, a former Mau Mau leader.

MRA Photo, Caux, Switzerland

'What's this place?' we asked. 'This is West Malling'
(in mid-Kent). 'Funny sort of airfield,' I commented,
'full of molehills.' 'Not moles,' he replied, 'unexploded
bombs; they've been going off all through the night.'
We jumped down into his hole, telephoned Marham
and requested to be re-fuelled.

I went and looked over the Wellington and decided
it was safe to fly on. A refueller arrived, manned by
some very nervous airmen. We had never been re-
fuelled so fast; then they were gone. We learned that
on the previous day a big raid by German bombers
flying towards London had been met by RAF fighters
over West Malling and had dumped their bombs
before turning back to France. The airfield had been
evacuated, its fighters sent elsewhere. Only this one
flying control officer had been left. We rumbled across
the airfield to take off, my heart in my mouth, fearing
our vibration might set off an explosion.

Back in the interrogation room at Marham our plots
and timings were carefully analysed. Another crew
had claimed to have hit the target factory and set it
on fire. It was probably the fire we had seen to the
south of us. The other Captain was a very experienced
pilot from civil aviation and he was convinced he had
hit the right place. We put a bold face on our story,
although I had doubts. To complicate matters, the
Group Air Vice-Marshal had telephoned to congratu-
late the station and added, 'There is an immediate
award of a Distinguished Flying Cross (DFC) in this,
please give me the name.' Both crews were bone weary
and it seemed impossible to decide who had hit the
right target. The Station Commander invited us to toss

a coin, and the other Captain won. I was glad of it, especially when, a few days later, he was shot down. His wife had something to show of his gallantry.

Operations over Europe became steadily more hazardous week by week as the Germans developed their air defence from the coast to Germany, with permanent sites for radar, searchlights, flak and night fighters with their elaborate control. One night, as we returned from a raid on the Ruhr, our rear-gunner reported that he could see a fighter following us. He had first reported its white downward recognition light (which helped his gunners on the ground.) Then he reported blue and gold lights in the cockpit and he could count two heads. I asked him to keep giving me their distance behind us, estimated with his gunsight, but on no account to fire. I reckoned our firing would give our enemy a pinpoint to aim at, and his cannons were much more deadly than our two Vickers guns firing at a head-on fighter. He crept up on us slowly. I turned left, he followed us. I turned right and dived, and again he followed us. It was clear he could not see us, but had some device by which he could follow us. Before the war I had exercised with ground operators who listened to aircraft approaching England for air defence purposes, and I had helped them to calibrate. In the course of doing this I heard a hint that there were other ways of picking up and fixing aircraft flying in. So I had a suspicion that this German fighter might be carrying similar equipment.

As we made our way to the Belgian coast we played a cat and mouse game. I could not throw him off and he did not have enough confidence to open fire. Finally I instructed the rear-gunner to aim, and, when the fighter came within 150 yards, to shout. At once I pulled the Wellington up into a high stall. We hung there on the engines, then fell out of the stall, to find that the fighter was about one hundred yards ahead of us. He immediately began hunting around to find us on his screen, but he couldn't see backwards. At the coast he dived away and we continued on our way to Marham.

Our Intelligence people appeared to be very interested in our report of this encounter. One hinted that this was a very early report of German airborne radar in use.

The RAF had its own disinformation campaign about radar. Before each sortie bomber aircrews were handed red lozenges - we called them cat's eyes - and were informed that they were carrots, to help us see better in the dark. After the war, I heard that the Germans, after many interrogations of shot-down crews, had put scientists to work to investigate the powers of the carrot, perhaps to explain their own bomber losses by night over Britain.

6

Malta Ahoy

One day in October 1940, one of our crews, hit by flak over the Ruhr, staggered back to Norfolk and crashed in the dark near the coast. My CO and I drove to see the crash and on to the hospital to see how the crew were. When we got back to Marham, after midnight, the sentry on the gate directed me urgently to the Station Operations Room. There the new Station Commander was hard at work organising a special operation in the Mediterranean. I had been selected to lead it. I was to take off to Malta in just sixteen hours time with six Wellingtons from Marham's two squadrons and six from Mildenhall's two squadrons. We were to attack a highly secret target in Italy and then return, our CO implied, in about ten days. Bed was forgotten, crews were selected and called out to start the preparations.

Very little seemed to be known at Marham about the facilities in Malta - what sort of an airfield it had, what navigational aids, what maintenance manpower, spares, bombs, ammunition, and so on. We sent signals of enquiry to Malta, but no replies had been received by the time we set off. As we collected items we weighed them and prepared loading tables in order to balance the aircraft about its centre of gravity. There came a point at which we were up to full load, yet there were still many items we felt we needed. So we hung them around the aircraft and crossed our fingers that the Wellingtons would get off the ground. I loaded a flash bomb and a camera. Others took canisters of incendiary bombs. We fitted long range tanks to the Wellingtons, but had no opportunity to test whether they worked or how to switch them. I threw in my portable typewriter - and how grateful we were for that later. We took the minimum of clothing, since we were to be away only ten days.

At midday we received a message that we must take maintenance airmen, who would go by sea. As the men marched back to the hangars from their midday dinner and came to a halt, I shouted out, 'Men stand fast. Flight Sergeant Sharpe, here, please.' Sharpe came forward. He was our best engineer. 'Flight,' I said, 'We're going away on a ten-day detachment with operations and will have twelve aircraft. How many airmen will you need? It must be an absolute minimum.' Sharpe pulled out a cigarette pack and figured on the back of it. 'I'll need 98, sir.' 'All we're allowed to take is 60, Flight, so you'd better pick the best you know.' He remonstrated with me and finally beat me up to 66. Then he called these men out from the ranks and sent them off to their billets to pack a small kit and assemble in two hours.

One of our gunner officers, Flying Officer Bitmead, who had just completed an operational tour, was told to take the party to Glasgow by train and see them on board a cruiser, which would take them full speed to Malta. A week or so later, the party reached Malta, together with Bitmead, who explained that the cruiser sailed before he could get ashore - a statement that none of us believed. So I appointed him Malta Squadron Adjutant, a much-needed official to organise our disparate unit and he performed the task well. Though he was 'off ops' Bitmead was to be found in a Wellington's rear turret on interesting sorties.

As my Squadron CO watched me climb aboard for our flight to Malta he remarked, 'Don't be surprised if you have to stay out there longer than ten days.' It was nine months before I got back to England, and many of my men were away for three years or more.

As we taxied out to take off, the sirens sounded and a few moments later a German bomber came in low to drop a stick of bombs across the end of the airfield, but apparently doing no harm. We had about 6,000 feet of grass for our take-off and we needed all of it, just scooting across the fence on the boundary. We climbed steadily for more than 100 miles before we reached 8,000 feet, our cruising altitude. I spotted a big oil fire on the ground, with what looked to me like incendiary bombs exploding.

When we reached Malta I was told that one of our two missing aircraft had struck a balloon in England and was burned out, with all killed. The second missing Wellington caused quite a stir. It carried on its bomb racks a highly secret cypher machine. The Captain had been told to dump it if in any trouble, so that it would be smashed to pieces. From the time of take-off nothing had been heard of the aircraft, nor had the Germans or Italians made any claim of shooting down an aircraft. It might have hit a mountain or come down in the sea. In Malta we were far too busy to investigate further. The stir died down, so perhaps somewhere someone heard enough to pacify the Intelligence staff.

On the flight from Marham to Malta the crew was Sergeant Alan Dyer as second pilot, Sergeant Michael Wiseman as navigator/bomb aimer, Sergeant J. Wallace McCulloch as wireless operator, Sergeant Stan Kent as rear gunner and Sergeant H. Adams as front gunner. All of them were excellent men of about my own age who had joined 115 Squadron about the same time as I did. Wiseman went on to photo reconnaissance all around the Mediterranean and completed 109 sorties in all. There can be few who did more sorties and survived. Dyer was killed on his second operational tour from England. Adams was killed over the western desert. Kent finished the war as a squadron leader flying assault gliders with the Army. McCulloch went on to air transport Liberators and survived two major crashes, one in Gibraltar and the second in South Wales.

As our Wellington flew across the French coast at Le Havre, flak opened up on us, bursting close. At that moment the engines coughed and faltered. It took us a moment to realise that the overload tank might be emptying and we needed to get back and adjust the valves of our regular tanks. The engines picked up and ran smoothly for the rest of the voyage.

We came into daylight near Sardinia. Our track was towards Cap Bon in Tunisia and we hoped the French in Bizerta, now under Vichy control, would not attack us. Then we set course to give a wide berth to the island of Pantelleria, where Italian fighters might be stationed, also keeping clear of Sicily. As we passed to the north of 'Pants' we suddenly saw an aircraft coming towards us, but much lower. We watched it until we realised it was a Wellington. At that moment the aircraft dived towards the sea, obviously having seen us and fearing an enemy. We arrived in Malta in eight and a half hours, landing on the larger airfield, Luqa. It seemed small to me, with its longest strip short for a loaded Wellington.

I went to Valletta, Malta's capital, to report to the Air Officer Commanding (A.O.C.), Air Vice-Marshal Samuel Maynard. His first question to me was, 'What have they sent you here for?' I told him what little I knew, principally the secret target that we were to attack. He said, 'That target is absolutely banned without the Prime Minister's personal say-so. I'll signal London.' I heard later that that target remained sacrosanct all through the war.

Maynard ordered an attack on the oil storage tanks in Naples docks, which provided fuel for the Italian navy. He wanted the operation carried out that very night, while we still had the advantage of surprise. We were to fly out to the west of Sicily and then, in a great V, to approach Naples as though we had flown from Britain. We would then only have enough fuel to return directly to Malta. We had a wild rush-around to find out what there was at Luqa and on the island to equip us for this operation. We shanghai'd anyone, Air Force, Navy, Army or civilian, who could be persuaded to help lift on bombs, arm guns, refuel or service aircraft. Since we were the first bomber force in Malta, and therefore the island's first opportunity to reply to the enemy in kind, many volunteers and much help was forthcoming.

I had grave doubts about our pilots finding the blacked-out island in the dark, with no navigational aids, and because the airfield was so small, I decided to take off around midnight in order to be back over Malta at dawn.

The operation was a success. My crews found Naples all lit up and patently unprepared for an attack by night. Towards the end of the raid some lights began to be dowsed and a few guns put up a barrage. Next morning a Maryland photo-reconnaissance aircraft from Malta took some excellent photos of the docks, showing several oil tanks heavily damaged.

I was clear that if we were to continue using Luqa, the airfield must be made safer for Wellingtons. The one long runway was 900 yards, with a grass over-run of about 400 yards. At its end, up wind, stood a 20-foot tall memorial chapel. As I sat in the Wellington's pilot seat, that chapel looked enormous. As I gained speed on take-off it seemed to grow larger and larger, and I barely cleared it. A watcher estimated that the clearance was about six feet. In this warmer air and the light winds the Wellington needed a longer run than in the UK. At night especially, our pilots were sorely tempted to pull their Wellingtons off too quickly, which could make them sink back to collide with the chapel.

I went at once to see the AOC, making the point

that if the chapel were not removed at once, one of our Wellingtons might do it, and provide the memorial chapel with more bodies. Perhaps my remark reached the Archbishop; in any case, the AOC and I were both surprised when he ordered its removal for the duration of the war. This involved marking each stone, so that it could be restored later. The bodies under the chapel had also to be disinterred.

The speed of the removal was also no doubt hastened by what happened during our second attack on Naples the next night. The A.V.M. ordered us to execute the same operation, flying west of Sicily. Conditions were perfect, with a mild zephyr of wind from the west. Since the island had no RAF operational staff I took charge of the whole arrangement, including seeing off each aircraft. I worked at the base of the control tower informing the Island's Joint Operations Room, where officers were controlling the searchlights, guns and radar. The first three Wellingtons got away normally. The fourth, flown by Sergeant Lewin, became airborne and then I saw his white tail light sink, recover and climb away. As the next aircraft was shaping up to take off I heard a great rumble to the west, near the ancient city of Rabat, in the hills. I saw a fire starting up in those hills, then heard small bangs, followed by a huge explosion, with pyrotechnics lacing the sky.

The next Wellington was successfully airborne, but as another took off, I watched its tail light disappear behind the chapel, sinking down into the valley beyond. There followed a horrible crunching noise, then mounting smoke and flames. I jumped to the telephone and spoke to the AOC, telling him I was halting the operation, and why. He agreed.

We learned later that Sergeant Lewin's Wellington had flown into a hill almost parallel with the ground and had broken up against the stone walls lining the tiny fields on top of the hill. As the crew jumped out a small fire started. Lewin found that his navigator was missing and realised he was somewhere in the aircraft.

So, despite the increasing fire, he climbed back into the broken fuselage, found his navigator and pulled him out. Then he lay on him as the bombs exploded. Both were unhurt. Lewin was awarded a George Cross for this act of gallantry. Sadly, he died later in a flying accident.

In the second crash, the Wellington ended up lying on the roof of a big house. The front part of the fuselage broke off and fell into a quarry, where it caught fire. All but one of the crew were in this section. A Maltese policeman looked down into the quarry and thought he saw a crewman trying to escape. He took a rope and with the aid of villagers lowered himself into the quarry, where he pulled out one of our men. For this he was awarded the British Empire Medal. Two British Army officers climbed up into the house below the body of the Wellington and rescued a number of children from their beds. The parents were killed. These officers were also decorated. In the morning the rear gunner was found asleep on the roof inside the wrecked fuselage and apparently not aware of what had happened. Beneath him, laid out in neat rows, were the bombs in their racks.

I immediately took steps to make take-offs less difficult. We lightened the Wellingtons by removing all
armour plate, reducing the crew by one gunner,
limiting fuel to half tanks and practising take-offs to
get the fastest lift into the air with safety. The removal
of the chapel was a big bonus.

It soon became clear that we were not going to
return to Marham. We became, in fact, a part of the
Middle East Command in Cairo, and we began calling
ourselves 'Somerville's Own', because this famous
Admiral, the Commander-in-Chief of the Navy in the
Mediterranean, sent us to attack the Italian Navy,
wherever Intelligence said it was skulking, in order to
drive it out to sea. Then the Admiral would chase it
into some other port. So we flew to raid Bari, Brindisi,
Messina and ports in Yugoslavia. When the Royal
Navy made their very successful attack on the Italian
fleet in Taranto we played a part by flare dropping
and diversions.

When I hurried off to Malta for the 'ten day' operation
I had no idea how strategic an island it was. During
the months our squadron was there Malta was the sole
base for the Navy and RAF in the 1500-mile stretch of
the Mediterranean, from Gibraltar to the Egyptian
border. Late 1940 was a crucial time in the Mediterranean. The Italian army was poised on the border,
preparing to invade Egypt. The British Army and
associated forces, under the command of General
Wavell, were also preparing to attack.

Malta was the refuelling point for all long range
aircraft flying to support Wavell. One of our important

tasks was to receive these single aircraft and speed them on their way. Early in December 1940, a complete squadron of Wellingtons, No 37 Squadron, landed en route to Egypt. Our AOC retained one Flight, commanded by Squadron Leader H. Murton, and briefed him and me on a special operation we were to conduct. He had received a very reliable report that a large concentration of Italian bombers had been assembled on the airfield at Castel Benito, behind Tripoli, in what is now Libya. It was believed that this force would be dispersed up the desert within the next twenty-four hours to support the advance against Wavell. The A.O.C. called for a strike to be made immediately and in daylight to be sure of finding and damaging the Italian aircraft. Murton and I demurred; we had never made a daylight attack with Wellingtons. Finally the A.O.C. struck a compromise: six of us would attack before dark and the other six would follow after sunset.

Murton led one flight of three Wellingtons. His plan was to fly round the west side of Tripoli and straight to Castel Benito. I led another three. My plan was to fly east of Tripoli, drop a few bombs on a fighter airfield there, to discourage them from taking off, and then go on to Castel Benito. The six Wellingtons following us would fly singly. We counted on surprise, since this would be the first taste of real war in this area of North Africa.

We set off in Vic formation, something we had never done before, hoping our rear gunners would defend our tails. We had had no time to replace our armour or work out together how we would man-

oeuvre. It was still daylight when the African coast
came into view. I felt much as I imagined I would feel
like walking down a high street without my clothes
on.

As we crossed the coastline, my navigator was lying
on the floor, looking for the fighter airfield below. He
could not see it. After our months of night bombing
we were not used to seeing brown and green countryside. I left my second pilot, Sergeant MacDougall, in
control and jumped down beside my navigator. At
6,000 feet we could identify nothing. I told the pilot
to steer for Castel Benito and I climbed up into the
astrodome to see how my wing aircraft had fared. To
my horror, neither of them was in sight. I at once
assumed they had been shot down, though I had seen
no sign of enemy activity. At that moment I spotted
Castel Benito coming up, and on the airfield a remarkable sight - line upon line of three-engined bombers,
drawn up as though for inspection. My guess was that
there were at least two hundred. Then, across their
front, I saw a cloud of dust moving - a fighter taking
off.

It was evident that I was the first Wellington on the
scene. Over the intercom I warned the crew of the
fighter's approach and told the pilot to turn to the
right and drop the bombs along the length of the
target. This he did. Then I caught sight of the Italian
bi-plane fighter climbing fast just ahead of us. I told
MacDougall to turn against the fighter's turn, the front
gunner to give him a burst and then dive the aircraft
to the ground and fly as low as possible at full throttle
for the coast.

Just as MacDougall rolled over to dive, the fighter
made his first attack. One moment I had a mask and
microphone on my face, the next it had disappeared,
one of his bullets must have hit it. The roll and dive
gave us such gravitational pull - G - that I could not
move. I was convinced that MacDougall had been
killed and we were diving into the desert. Not so: he
pulled her out so close to the ground we were blowing
up a cloud of dust from the desert. The fighter came
in again and again and his bursts hit the Wellington.
Fortunately he was inexperienced and came in too
close before he fired. Many of his shells missed or hit
us in the wings. He seemed to be scared of hitting the
ground, so his attacks were flat and slow. Our rear
gunner returned fire until he was wounded.

In my astrodome I could watch everything, but
without my microphone there was no way I could
intervene. I shouted directions but no one heard. As
more shells flew at us, like a red stream, I decided I
was a target and crouched down on the floor. No
sooner had I crouched than a shell burst inside the
fuselage not far from my feet. I could not bear not to
see what was happening, so I got to my feet and I
turned sideways, reckoning I made a narrower target.

MacDougall was doing well; his sideways skids
threw the fighter off aim. Finally the fighter climbed
away into the semi-darkness executing barrel rolls -
victory rolls in his mind, I suspect. Then we saw him
firing in the half-light at another plane. I hoped he
would soon run out of ammunition.

I could see white smoke pouring out of one of our
wings and black smoke out of the other. Sheets of

fabric, which had covered the wings, now streamed
out like flags behind them. I reckoned the white smoke
was petrol escaping from a badly damaged self-sealing
tank and the black smoke might be oil leaking. At that
point we dodged round a small hill capped by a fort.
I saw Italian soldiers staring down at us, then turning
to run for their guns. Then we were over the sea. We
climbed for height, fully expecting that our engines
would fail or that other damage might force us down.
We had to get our wounded rear gunner out of his
turret in case we ditched. It was not easy to move him,
especially as he was in much pain, and I could not
give him morphia - lifting a sleeping man into a dinghy
would have been too difficult.

The engines kept churning and the aircraft flew
normally, but it was obvious that it was badly damaged. As Malta loomed up, in pitch dark, we radioed
that we were damaged and had a wounded man
aboard. As I took the controls I prayed that our
hydraulic system would work. The wheels went down,
but not the flaps, but somehow I got her down along
the gooseneck flares and swung round on the grass
near the boundary, coming to a stop without further
damage. The Wellington proved to be a write-off, but
it did provide us with a lot of spares.

The next Wellington to return had been shot up by
a fighter and made a belly landing on our one runway.
I rushed around to find men and lorries to haul it
away, as more and more Wellingtons began to stack
up, circling the island. The later crews were euphoric.
When they arrived over Castel Benito they had found
fires burning. The only defence was heavy machine

guns at the corners of the airfield and these were put out of action by our air gunners. Then they flew up and down the lines of Italian bombers, spraying them with bullets, as though practice shooting at a ground target.

HQ told us next day that a reliable report indicated that 109 Italian bombers were destroyed or damaged - more than half the bomber force preparing to fly up the desert to support the attack by Marshal Graziani. Two days later, General Wavell went on the attack and captured the entire Italian army.

I solved the mystery of the disappearance of my two wing aircraft. They saw we had flown right across the middle of the fighter airfield at Tripoli, and when it was clear that we had not seen it, the two aircraft had turned back to dive bomb before continuing to Castel Benito. Months later I acquired a Middle East Command Mention in Despatches for this attack.

We continued our night raids on Naples, and on one of them we encountered very accurate flak, different from the colourful but inaccurate Italian anti-aircraft fire. All of us had experienced German flak over Europe and we were convinced that now it had arrived in Naples. We reported this to Intelligence in Malta, which was largely a naval organisation, and they questioned our conclusion. Next day, the photo reconnaissance plane over Naples experienced the same accurate flak and, further, their photos showed stores marshalled along the docks in precise rows, nothing like the usual Italian haphazard fashion. This convinced us that there were German preparations to move to Tripoli. Then one of our aircraft reported

accurate flak coming out of a merchant ship steaming
southward. We hoped this evidence would convince
Intelligence to warn our forces in the Western Desert.

Malta was of importance for more than the refuelling
of bombers and raids on enemy supplies and aircraft.
A few days after our attack on Castel Benito, a British
convoy was reported approaching Malta from the
west. It was being escorted by HMS *Illustrious*, one of
our largest aircraft carriers, and other naval ships. The
carrier was about to turn back near Pantelleria island,
when she was attacked by dozens of German Ju 87
Stukas and other aircraft. She was badly damaged and
it was decided to bring her on to Malta for repair, along
with the convoy. Some of the merchant ships got
through safely and were unloaded with maximum
speed in order to deploy their cargoes of anti-aircraft
guns, ammunition and army stores to defend the
carrier and other naval vessels. Malta lay only fifty
miles from enemy shores and the ships were a prize
target for bombing.

The Germans mounted heavy raids and some ships
were sunk as they lay alongside the Valletta docks.
From our vantage point on Luqa airfield we could see
the whole dockyard laid out below us, the carrier
alongside the repair yard and the guns on the fortif-
ications of Valletta defending the area. The battle went
forward before our eyes. The Maltese population
crowded the battlements to watch the raids, ignoring
the falling shrapnel, shell cases and bullets from the
German aircraft. When the pom-poms on the carrier
and the docks - the Navy called them Hell's pianos -

began rapid firing, the crowd would go almost berserk, cheering and gesticulating like a football crowd.

One man in particular stands out in my memory of that battle. 'Jock' Joughin was the civilian engineer who ran the repair side of the dockyard, with the title, The Constructor. I had come to know him well and to admire him. He was past retirement age, but had been kept on in Malta because of the start of the war. Very deaf, he carried an ancient hearing aid, the size of a small suitcase. He had taken the trouble to learn some Maltese, something few British did in those days, and was clearly much beloved by the Maltese artificers and shipyard workers, who spoke little English. As soon as the *Illustrious* docked she was surveyed and the dead and wounded taken off. The gun crews remained to fight off attacks. The damage on the decks and below was considerable and must be patched up before the ship could sail to a fully equipped dockyard.

At a conference, I was told, there were some who shook their heads; they could not see how the repairs could be made under the attacks from the Sicily-based German Stukas. Not so Joughin. He was adamant he would get the ship away within fourteen days, if everything was done to protect her from further damage - a tall order. He concentrated on the task of plugging the under-water damage, and for this he needed divers.

The first attacks on the carrier caused many bombs to fall among the workers' homes in the dock perimeter. Naturally, the dockers set about digging out their homes and their casualties, and work in the docks stopped. Jock hurried through the streets urging them

to leave their homes and shelters and get to work on
the *Illustrious* right away. Amazingly, they did so.
Jock's divers had many hours of work under water
around the carrier. They knew that the concussion
from a bomb falling in the harbour could kill a diver.
Jock convinced them to go down by telling them, 'I
will sit in your pump boat and hold your life-line. If I
sense danger I will bring you up and we will be clear
of the ship before there is an attack.' To these deeply
Catholic workmen Joughin was a man of God and they
had full faith in him. Malta's air raid warning system
gave at most a twelve minute warning of the enemy
leaving Sicily, insufficient time to bring up the divers
and get them to a safe distance. For two days Jock sat
in the boat and held the lines while the men worked
below. All the time they were below there was no raid.
Only when he had decided to bring them up and they
were rowing ashore did the alarm sound. The *Illustrious* was away within fourteen days.

On the third morning of attacks on *Illustrious* the
sirens sounded and our men went to the slit trenches
and shelters. Our new adjutant, who had arrived with
the convoy, another officer and I stood outside to
watch the attack start on the carrier. Suddenly I
realised that the Stukas had passed the ship and were
overhead. They were beginning to peel off into vertical
dives and I heard their front guns firing. They seemed
to be coming straight for the three of us. I dived into
a shallow slit trench which had only just begun to be
dug. It was about three feet deep. My adjutant landed
on top of me and the other officer on top of him. The
ground heaved, dust fell in on us as more than seventy

heavy bombs exploded nearby with an appalling bang that seemed to rumble on indefinitely. Then all was quiet, except for the bark of the Bofors guns around the airfield and the heavy artillery in the valley below. The clouds of dust drifted slowly away. It was, for me, a shattering experience. My new adjutant said, 'You look very frightened, sir.' 'By God, I am very frightened,' I replied. 'I never thought the CO would be frightened.' 'Well, I was.'

The gunners told us they had counted 76 Stukas dive bombing the airfield in about three minutes. They had shot down several and others were clearly damaged.

I went out onto the field. There was the clang of galvanised iron flapping in the wind. Nearly all our buildings were devastated and, more important, there were some enormous craters in the runways, big enough to swallow a double-decker bus. No one could land or take off on that field. To restore it to operations looked to me a mammoth task of several days. How to do it and where to start? At that moment, around the perimeter taxi track came a motor cycle and sidecar, driven by a huge Army Sergeant-Major. Sitting beside him was a small, dapper Lieutenant-Colonel.

The Colonel didn't seem to notice me, but leapt out and ran up the pile of rubble on which I was standing. He surveyed the scene, then remarked to nobody in particular, 'A bit dusty.' And again, 'Very big holes.' 'Yes,' I said, in a slightly hostile voice. He pondered some more, then turned to me and said, 'I have 230 men. I shall need thirty for fatigues (camp duties). You can have the rest to fill those holes.' He looked at his watch and added, 'They've gone to lunch now; it'll take thirty minutes, then they'll be here.' At which, he hurried down the rubble, sat himself in the sidecar and was driven away. I didn't know his name, what his unit was, or where they came from. I did notice that he wore a cravat instead of a tie, with a fox-hunting pin in it.

I hurried into our camp to find the Station Warrant Officer. He was superintending the digging of some poor dead airman out of a slit trench. I told him, 'There are going to be 200 soldiers arriving in thirty minutes to fill the holes in the airfield. I want every soldier matched by an airman. If necessary, enlist the air-crews.' I was interrupted by a message ordering me to report to Headquarters in Valletta. When I returned an hour later an amazing sight met my eyes. Back on the pile of rubble stood the little Colonel, with his Sergeant-Major. As I watched, he pointed his swagger stick and away rushed the RSM. Around the airfield were some 400 men, bathed in sweat. Soldiers were attacking the holes with their trenching tools like men possessed. Among them were men in blue, some slowly digging, some lying prostrate, evidently run off their feet.

As I clambered up beside the Colonel, he said with enthusiasm, 'Get your men out of here and on to those planes and get them ready. We're going to get them off the ground soon and knock hell out of those b....s. From now on, your men keep the planes flying and my gunners'll see that they can take off.'

From that day onward, whenever we had a blitz and bomb damage, the Army appeared spontaneously to do the donkey work to make the airfield fit for battle. Later on the soldiers helped us with the arming of aircraft with belts of bullets, hoisted up bombs, aided with refuelling and many other tasks that our men could not have coped with on their own, as life became increasingly hectic. That Colonel's initiative was the start of a new teamwork between the Services which, in my opinion, was a decisive factor in keeping Malta a fighting base through the long siege and on until the invasion of Sicily.

That very evening we were airborne and found the Stukas on Catania airfield in Sicily. It seemed that we were not expected. The aircraft were parked in neat lines along the runway. They were highly visible in a bright moonlit night and we bombed them heavily. A photo next day indicated some thirty Stukas destroyed. The German flak was intense and accurate. One Wellington was hit and lost with all its crew. A second was damaged and had to make a landing in the sea. By an extraordinary chance a British submarine was nearby and was able to pick up the crew from their dinghy unhurt. As I flew over the target I put my head forward to concentrate on the instruments, to fly accurately for the bomb aimer, and so that I would not see the shell bursts, some of them very close. Then a shell burst right beside us. I sat up and found a hole in my side window and another in the opposite window, in line with where my head would normally have been.

Once the *Illustrious* had left, the Germans made a dead set for Luqa airfield, attacking us both with bombers and fighters almost daily. Their fighters especially concentrated on our Wellingtons, using their front guns to try to damage them in their pens, big stone U-shaped walls some 15 feet high. The pens gave wonderful protection, except on their open side.

Malta was becoming increasingly busy as a refuelling point. Almost every morning now we received reinforcement aircraft from Britain, mostly Wellingtons being flown out to the Middle East. Most of them we sent on to Egypt, a few we were allowed to keep to replace our losses on the ground. We could only fly at night. In daylight, even a short air test was almost impossible, with the German fighters flying around the island. During my last three months on Malta we lost close to fifty Wellingtons on the ground. During the same period, as far as we could judge, the Germans lost more than that. And of course they lost their crews with them, either killed or made prisoner. Our crews, at least, were on Malta, available for another day.

The Germans were a much more dangerous enemy than the Italians. Before the Germans arrived we had regular bombing raids by the Italian air force. They flew over in their three- engined bombers in a nice formation at about 14,000 feet, usually at precisely 11 o'clock. They aimed at the intersection of the runways and, as they rarely got the windspeed and direction exactly right, the bomb craters would form a nice group one or two hundred yards from their aiming point. The craters were small and rarely on the runways. So consistent were the Italians that we used to gather on the edge of the airfield, some 500 yards away, to watch the performance.

When the Germans began arriving, it was a very different matter. To keep aircraft flying by night we had to work on them by day. Our ground crews were made up of a small number of RAF technicians, the ground staff of a Naval Swordfish squadron, mostly sailors, and an increasing number of Maltese dockyard workers, who were civilians and for the most part did not speak much English. Whenever a German sweep was picked up by radar the sirens were sounded. The airfield workers hurried into the excellent deep shelters near the pens, the servicemen into one and the Maltese into another. With the constant sweeps, it became more and more difficult to get work done on the aircraft.

In the hope that we could build a trust that would keep the Maltese working longer before diving into their shelter, I asked our men if they would go into the same shelter with the Maltese. There was some reluctance, but in the end some did, and soon made friends. More followed. Then I asked the Maltese if they would allow me to post an aircrew to be a look-out, sitting up on the wing, who would warn them when there was real danger. In this way a lot more work was accomplished. Also, some real co-operation developed between servicemen and Maltese. In peacetime, in those days, any fraternisation between the two was rare. In a few weeks together in the shelters friendships grew and men began to visit homes in their time off. It meant a lot to both.

Our men became highly critical of the anti-aircraft gunnery. The shell bursts were behind enemy aircraft and had no effect on their run up. I decided to do something about it. I sat down and wrote a memo on what it was like from the pilot's point of view, to be shot at by anti-aircraft guns - what frightened me and made me jink and turn, and what did not. Shells which burst ahead of me shook me; shells bursting behind me did not worry me, because I didn't see them. Our AA gunners were strictly limited in the number of rounds they could fire, so it was important that they create the maximum effect with what they had, if not destroying an aircraft, at least disturbing the enemy pilot and bomb aimer.

I offered the memo to a gunner friend. A couple of days later, I received a phone call from an Army Brigadier, inviting me to have dinner with him. It was an excellent repast. At its conclusion he said, 'I've been reading your memo on what it's like to be shot at. I think it's excellent. In fact, I've had copies made and sent to every AA battery on the island. But I know my chaps; they don't read what HQ sends them. Do you think you could come and talk to one or two of my batteries, please?' I gladly accepted, and in the end found myself whisked to twenty gun sites all over the island.

At each, the gunners, British and Maltese, would demonstrate their gun drill; then I would talk along the lines of my memo. At the end there would be questions and inevitably someone would ask the burning question in the minds of gunners, 'Please, sir, why is it that the RAF fighters never seem to attack the bombers?' I saw many red faces among battery COs when this question was asked. I thanked them for their question and explained that Malta had at best six Hurricanes and two Gladiators, if all were service-able at any one time. There were no replacements in sight, so we could not afford to lose even one. As long as these fighters were flying around at bomber height, ready to cut out a straggler, and always threatening to attack, they were sufficient to divert the Italians from a careful attack. I explained that we had a 'force in being', a good military principle.

These visits of mine seemed to have a dual effect, to stop Army criticism of the RAF, and to improve the AA gunnery. They also led to the AA inviting our aircrews to visit them on their days off, to get a change of air and interest, which was helpful to our morale. However, when the submariners of the Royal Navy, who helped us with accommodation when we were bombed out, offered to give our aircrews a 'toot' around the island in one of their submarines, not one man volunteered. 'Too dangerous' was their private response.

One day, the Germans flattened our officers' mess. We were offered the use of a beautiful house in Valletta, built by the Knights of St John as one of their Castiles, several hundred years ago. The house lent itself to a much more gracious level of living than did the hutments we had left. So I set about arranging mess evenings for our officers. These encouraged them to smarten up their clothes and their manners and they found themselves enjoying it more than they expected. The evenings also seemed to help men avoid heavy drinking, gambling and looking for the tarts in the bazaar. These were all understandable reactions to the stress which all of us were experiencing from the daily dangers of enemy attack on the ground and in the air.

A symptom of that stress which all my aircrew had in common was the 'twitch', as we called it. This was a physical manifestation, shown by flickering eyelids, a nervous tic in the corner of the mouth, headache pains and often bowel upsets. Sometimes hands tended to shake noticeably, especially on take-off or approaching a target. Each chap had his variant. All of them had come from Europe, where they had completed an operational tour of up to thirty raids. When taken off operations in Europe they were given a Wellington to take to the Middle East - 'Mystical East', as some thought, and 'Muddle East', as most called it when they got there. On their landing in Malta en route they found themselves shanghai'd into the Malta Wellington Squadron to fly out of a blacked-out island, on long raids over the sea and with no alternative airfield on which to land on their return. It could be highly stressful.

I soon decided that one of my main responsibilities as CO was to convince my captains, and then the rest of my aircrews, that each was the man for the job; that their strength lay within themselves, not in a bottle or other means of hiding or suppressing fear. I was frank that all of us were afraid and that together we could beat our fear. I could not promise them a definite number of raids before they came off operations again, as we had no idea when replacements might arrive. They could see the war right over their heads, a very personal war, and they must assume that they would fight that war until they died, or their CO took them out of it. Meantime, each was the man for the job, and he could accomplish it. Fortunately we had very few casualties, and none which remained a mystery.

My second task with the aircrew was how to make life interesting, companionship a pleasure, and how to help men to be concerned with one another. I started with games in the mess. Mah Jong was especially popular; I have seen foursomes sit up all night playing it. They also enjoyed Bridge, Peggity and many other games. I encouraged our officers to take an interest in their airmen and associate with the sergeants, many of whom were aircrew. And I made myself available to walk around the airfield with individuals, to encourage them to talk about their fears, their dreadful nightmares (which I, too, had at times), and their twitch. It seemed to help them, and me, to be freed from the grip of their fears, and to reinforce their determination to acquit themselves gallantly - which they did.

One day, the new adjutant said to me, 'Do you know there are eleven of the aircrew who don't drink, and fifteen who don't smoke?' (My memory is hazy about the exact figures, and in those days nearly everyone smoked.) I replied with some surprise, 'Really? Why do you think that is?' 'Because you don't do either.' It was a new idea to me, but as I thought about it, I understood that the fellows in my squadron were alive longer because they were not unnecessarily brave and their reactions were sharper than men in other squadrons who lived a more indulgent life.

One of my responsibilities, which the crews seemed to appreciate, was to be in the operations room in

Valletta whenever our aircraft was operating in and out of the island. To find the blacked-out island, with enemy in the vicinity, required considerable trust between the aircrew in the air and the ground forces - RAF, Army and Navy who worked searchlights, radar and the lights on the airfield. It was like conducting a great orchestra. Then on many dawns I had the task of conning in new crews, flying from Britain and keeping them from being intercepted by the enemy fighters who patrolled off Malta. These crews were often tired and insecure. They did not know us and why we instructed them to do as we did.

I quickly learned, with these new crews, to jump on any trouble hard and fast. Once we got them down on the ground they sometimes let their hair down in riotous ways. One crew I had brought in, who had only just avoided an interception, though they didn't realise it, immediately sallied into Valletta to relieve their feelings in a very heavy drinking session. They were rounded up in an obstreperous state outside HQ and brought back to me. I told the crew, 'You will leave here for the Western Desert at 6 a.m. tomorrow. You do not fit in here.' I saw them off.

Perhaps a month later we received reinforcements from Egypt and among them was the same crew. 'Back you go,' I said. They pleaded with me, telling me how horrible they found the desert to be. I gave them twenty-four hours to integrate. The captain was so pleased, he took his crew into Valletta to celebrate. Later that night I was in bed when I heard a shot fired in the passageway outside. Further shots followed. I counted six, then leapt out of bed and went into the passageway - no sign of anyone. I walked until I came to that captain's room. I went in and found him in bed and pretending to be asleep. I ordered him out of bed; he was fully clothed. I took his pistol and smelt it. 'Off the ground by 6 am,' I said, 'and don't come back until you accept to live the way my chaps do.'

Most men seemed to catch the secret within twenty-four hours of arriving; that in our squadron one did not drink oneself silly, smoke to excess or poodle fake with the harlots. It was a regime without spoken instructions, and yet the majority agreed with it and observed it. One consequence was an excellent team spirit.

Not long before I left Malta, I had an encounter which helped relieve the tension of my duties. One day, Flight Sergeant Sharpe came into my office and said, 'You have a visitor, sir, an Armaments Inspector.' I could not believe an Armaments Inspector would come to such a dangerous place as Malta, where every rule in his books was being broken daily to contend with the conditions of war. Into the hut stepped my cousin, Peter Fidelis Foss. He had been, like me, a short service officer before the war and had then gone into Armaments Inspection. 'Sorry about our breaches of the armaments rules,' I told him, after we'd exchanged greetings. 'Conditions here are a *force majeure*.' He responded, 'Yes. I've seen it all and I understand. But that's not why I'm here. Did you know you have an Aunt on the island - Aunt Rose Foss? She runs a school in Sliema for officers' children. If you can get some transport, I'll take you to see her.'

We found Aunt Rose, for many years headmistress of Chiswick House School for officers' children. She was there throughout the war and nothing would deter her from her duty to educate the children, even when she could no longer assemble them and instead had to go to their homes one by one. When a land mine exploded near the school while I was visiting, she shook like a leaf, but her one concern was for the children. Aunt Rose was the first of my father's nine brothers and sisters whom I met as an adult. She opened my eyes to the Foss family and gave me a wholly new picture of them. After the war, when I went looking for Fosses, Aunt Rose's word pictures and addresses helped me to find and enjoy them.

7

Our Client - the Prime Minister

Malta and our airfield continued to be heavily blitzed
during the last months of 1940 and into 1941. It reached
the point when our squadron, now designated No 148
Squadron, only had two Wellingtons fit to fly. Middle
East HQ decided to withdraw us to Egypt. In April
1941, the majority of our aircrew and some of our
maintenance men were shipped to Alexandria by the
fast steaming freighter S.S. *Breconshire*. This gallant
ship, which dashed unescorted between Egypt and
Malta, was Malta's only supply line at that time. Every
voyage, a round trip of six days, could have been her
last. From time to time convoys of ten to fifteen ships,
escorted by naval vessels, tried to fight their way from
Gibraltar to Malta, but the loss of ships was very great.
My younger brother Denis was in one of the convoys,
soon after I left Malta. Only one quarter of the
merchant ships reached the island. His ship lay in
Malta for several months before making a run for it
and somehow arrived safely in Gibraltar.

I had been promoted to acting Wing Commander.
I also had a recurrence of internal trouble at the time
I was due to leave Malta, probably aggravated by

tiredness and stress from the six months fighting in Malta and the operational tour in Europe before that. The doctor marked me as sick and advised that I be flown to Egypt for treatment. A bed was fixed up for me in one of the two airworthy Wellingtons. The crew were ordered to leave at midnight, fly down the Mediterranean eastwards until abreast of the German front line near El Alamein, then turn due south so that the British defence could identify us as a friendly aircraft, posing no threat to Cairo or Alexandria. Once south of Cairo, the crew could turn east again and fly to land at Kabrit, on the Suez Canal.

As we flew through the night I slept and awoke suddenly in the first glimmer of light. I sat up in bed to meditate, as I did every morning, and soon began to feel that all was not well in the cockpit forward. I was only a passenger on this flight, and although I was their commanding officer, it was not done to interfere with the crew. I looked out and noted that we were flying over desert at about 4,000 feet. The pilot and navigator were in the cockpit, holding a map, and apparently trying to identify somewhere on the ground. My hunch was that they were lost.

I went forward to the navigator's table and looked through his written log and his working on the chart. I worked through it again and my conclusion was that we had turned south behind the German lines and that our track was taking us straight towards an oasis where I believed German fighters were stationed. I asked the wireless operator to get a fix or bearing from the Suez D/F station. He looked startled and told me they were ordered to observe wireless silence on this stage of the trip. However, I insisted and he did so. The bearing he received, laid out on the chart with the other data, confirmed my view that we were behind enemy lines. I hastily wrote a chit to the Captain, asking if one of them would come back and see me in the chart position. The navigator came and I showed him what I had learnt. Then I returned to bed. Shortly afterwards he came back to assure me that all was now well - we were now behind the British lines. He thanked me.

In Cairo I was given a medical examination, marked unfit and despatched to a troopship loading in Suez for a return trip to England. The S.S. *Cameronia* was old, built for the North Atlantic route. We were loaded with several hundred sick, many of them mentally ill, wives and children, and 1200 Italian prisoners of war. I was probably the third senior officer of the forces aboard. Since the Mediterranean was closed to us, we had to go around Africa via Kenya, South Africa, and Sierra Leone, West Africa, and on to Gibraltar and Glasgow. The voyage took three months.

I took life very quietly, enjoying my visits in Mombasa, Durban, East London, Cape Town, looking up friends in each place. When we reached Freetown, Sierra Leone, we lay at anchor for nearly three weeks, looking at the green countryside, because it was rumoured that a German submarine was waiting outside and we could not move until the Navy had dealt with it. We also joined a convoy there. A number of seamen, rescued from open boats, were added to our already crowded ship, and our mental cases rose steeply. I was told that more than a hundred men had to be put into straight jackets. On almost our last day at Freetown, a tug was found to convey several hundred of us to the shore for a walk through an African village to break the monotony. Off Gibraltar we had a different diversion, when we were attacked by a German Condor, whose bombs slightly damaged our stern. A Hurricane was catapulted off to chase it away. One excitement for me in a dull voyage was to be invited to be the defending officer at three Courts Martial. I got all three men off.

During the voyage I felt the urge to write a training pamphlet, which I called 'How to find Malta in the Dark.' When I reported on arrival in London to the Air Ministry, I left the manuscript with a Personnel Officer. I explained that we had been losing one aircraft in four flying to Malta - a casualty rate higher than that sustained by Bomber Command on operations over Germany. If only crew would read the pamphlet, I told him, we would not have such a casualty rate. In due course the pamphlet was published under a much more mundane title and marked 'Secret,' which considerably limited its use.

Submitting the pamphlet, however, made an immediate impact on my own future. After being marked fit for office duty and sent off for a week's leave, I was instructed to report to the Air Ministry, Bush House, London, to the Assistant Director of Organisation, Ferrying - ADO(F), a Wing Commander Hugh Fraser. I found a young, fine-looking officer expecting me. He sat me down and said, 'I'm told you feel strongly about the way aircraft are being sent out to the Middle East.' 'Strongly,' I replied, 'I feel that whoever is responsible is little short of a murderer. Certainly I feel strongly.' I noticed a slight flush on Fraser's face, so I added, 'Where do you come in on this?' He responded, 'Well, in the way you put it, I'm the murderer.'

Fraser went on to tell me the whole history of how Equipment had begun to fly out new aircraft without any arrangements for training crews or giving them practice. Nor were they given any operational directions. The Air Staff had known nothing about this method of delivery. The RAF Inspector-General had reported on these losses and particularly on the losses of reinforcement fighters to Malta, and insisted that there must be an operational set-up created to handle this growing movement. That was why ADO(F) had just come into being in the Air Ministry.

Fraser said he had been in the Air Ministry since the start of the war, though he had tried hard to get out and onto operations. He knew the Air Ministry and its ways. What he needed was someone with experience of this type of operations who would work with him. He paused and with a rather apologetic look added, 'I have a Squadron Leader post to fill. Would you consider dropping your Wing Commander stripe to take that post and help me?'

If it means getting crews out there alive, I thought to myself, it doesn't seem much of a price to pay, so I said readily, 'I'd be glad to work with you.' It proved to be one of the most important decisions of my life. We became a good team and enjoyed one another's company. Later, he arranged for me to take the short course at the RAF Staff College, which I found invaluable.

One day Fraser was taken ill in his office and carried out to hospital. I was instructed to take over and to put up a Wing Commander stripe again, this time as ADO(F). When Fraser recovered, he was put on operations. Sadly, he was killed on his first sortie.

As ADO(F), I found I was managing a unique branch. We were directly in touch with our small units in Cornwall, Gloucestershire and Ayrshire. We were directly controlling the movements of new aircraft coming from Canada and going to the Middle East and beyond through wireless stations at Gloucester and Prestwick. We made decisions while aircraft were in flight. This was foreign to the concept of the Air Ministry whose function was to set policies and make plans. The execution was then carried out by Commands, Groups and Stations.

My immediate boss was the Director General of Organisation who had a large department whose function was planning and co-ordination of supply - personnel, equipment, movements and much more. The Department lived in an atmosphere of being eighteen months ahead of the war.

ADO(F) came into being in 1941 because new aircraft had to be got to war zones quickly. It was the function of Equipment to provide new aircraft. In the past Movements would have shipped them by sea. Now some one had to respond to requests from overseas, bring together aircraft, aircrew in their variety, equipment for the flight, and offer a modicum of training to help get the aircraft delivered there. ADO(F) was really an air staff barnacle on the bottom of the supply ship! Almost no one wanted to know us to start with, apart from the Equippers who were glad to have this responsibility taken off their backs. By the time we were accepted a re-organisation (in 1943) in the Air Ministry created an Air Staff branch and ADO(F) ceased to exist.

ADO(F) directed a unit in Dorval, Montreal, Canada, from which the new American aircraft were despatched, usually with ferry crews. Prestwick was the arrival point where aircraft were handed over to Equipment and the ATA, the civilian internal delivery service. This transatlantic route was largely manned by civilian ferry crews, mainly American and Canadian, who were flown back to Dorval in Liberators of British Overseas Airways Corporation.

For deliveries to the Middle East and beyond, aircraft were usually assembled at Kemble, Gloucester. Then, after crew training, the aircraft were taken to Newquay in Cornwall and from there flown to Gibraltar, Malta and onward.

This became the routine, but at first each fly-out had to be 'lashed-up' with whatever we could arrange. In our ADO(F) office were three experienced men from Air France and Imperial Airways who handled the North Atlantic ferrying crews. These men taught me a lot, for I knew nothing about transport flying operations, or how to handle the civilian American aircrew.

The first task Fraser gave me, on joining the branch, was to arrange for three RAF fighter squadrons to fly

to Murmansk in northern Russia. I scarcely knew
where Murmansk was, what sort of weather prevailed
at that time of year, what airfields there were, what
flying aids, what translators, what equipment could be
found locally and, very important, what feeding and
accommodation there would be for aircrew and airmen. Naturally, the unit commanders wanted to know
all this information, just as I had done when I took
out the Malta Wellington Squadron. They flew off and
I heard precisely nothing of what happened to them,
even if and when they arrived.

I had begun to learn some of the intricacies of
dealing with the military attachés at the Russian
Embassy, also how to keep sweet and use many other
branches of the Air Ministry, who became involved
one way and another with providing our branch with
what was needed. No sooner was that piece of paper
work completed than another urgent job was thrown
at us and I had to switch my mind to that, hoping that
all was well with its predecessor. To my amazement I
found myself being treated as an expert by other
Ministry people.

Another early task was to deliver to the Middle East
a new type of transport aircraft, the Bombay. After
much delay, we sent off the first three, with the request
that the crews be returned to the UK to take out the
next batch. Nothing was heard from the Middle East
for months, except signals urging us to deliver the rest
of the aircraft quickly. Then, one day, crewmen began
to arrive back. They told us they had been sent across
Africa to Ghana to catch a ship. Since they had no
priority and no official orders, they had to hang

around for months in Ghana. Most of them contracted tropical diseases common there and by the time they returned they were not fit enough to make the journey again.

It became crystal clear to me that once a crew had made a delivery, the experience they had gained was invaluable for subsequent flights. They had begun to become a specialised crew - a Ferry Crew, such as we had on the North Atlantic. It was usual at that time to send out complete crews, ready to go into battle. We called this movement a Reinforcement. After completing the flight and gaining valuable experience from it, the crew was often broken up into holding units to replace casualties in squadrons.

This need to return ferry pilots was reinforced by other needs - to transport without delay Very Important Persons (VIPs), crucial supplies, documents and mail. They led me to push for the establishment of a flight to provide for such services. We instituted such a flight (No 1425 Flight) at Lyneham, Wiltshire, with three Liberators to shuttle between Cairo and England. It proved so valuable to all the Services, as well as to government, that it was expanded into a squadron, No 511 Squadron, at Lyneham. It was equipped with Liberator I's, one of the early lease-lend bombers from the United States, which had proved unsuitable for combat, mainly because it had no self-sealing fuel tanks. But it was very suitable for us, the longest range aircraft we had, and with some modifications for passenger comfort, right for the Atlantic and Mediterranean roles.

This was the unheralded start of an entirely new side of the RAF, long distance transport of passengers and goods to maintain communications between the theatres of war. Someone in the Air Ministry circulated a file inviting each branch to define its scope and role. I wrote in this file that ADO(F) was responsible for all overseas ferrying, for reinforcement with new aircraft and for air transport. My investigations had revealed that the only Air Ministry branch which claimed air transport as its role was the Civil Aviation Department, then located in Bristol. On enquiry I learned that they did not consider their responsibilities included military air transport; they said theirs related to BOAC and KLM and, of course, to planning for the return of peacetime aviation.

I received the impression that the Civil Aviation Department was, in fact, licking its wounds received at the hands of the RAF. In 1940, when the British Army was retreating to Dunkirk and Calais, there were urgent demands that supplies be dropped to the beleaguered men. Several BOAC crews were persuaded to fly over in their Hannibal civil airliners, which cruised at around 90 mph, with their cabin doors removed, to throw down bags of ammunition and supplies. They were given no means of communication with the ground troops, little information about their exact location, and no air protection. The pilots were given no assurances that their flying contracts covered the war risks they were being invited to undertake.

Afterwards there was some heavy recrimination and, as always, someone had to be blamed for what

went wrong and it proved to be the people in the Civil
Aviation Department. With this background it was no
surprise that Civil Aviation backed away from any part
in military air transport, leaving the door open for our
little branch to lay claim to responsibility for that field.

Not long afterwards, I was involved in an incident
which led to another important step being taken in
the creation of a many-sided air transport command.
One night, asleep in London, I was called to the
telephone. 'This is the Duty Officer in the War Room,'
said a voice. 'Can you come to the Air Ministry and
speak to me on a scrambler phone?' On the scrambler
(which precluded eavesdropping) I learnt that a BOAC
Clipper flying-boat was in the air on passage from
Bermuda direct to England. The Civil Aviation Department had telephoned the War Room asking that the
aircraft be given assistance to fly in to Milford Haven,
Wales, through the defences of Britain. On board were
VIPs and this had the highest priority. After receiving
this call from Bristol, the War Room had searched the
'bible' to learn which Air Ministry branch was responsible for air transport and found ADO(F).

Between 1 am and midday I built up a file almost
as thick as a book. For example, our Gloucester radio
station and control needed to know what radio fre-
quencies the flying-boat worked on, its call signs, its
facilities to cypher, its understanding of how to approach a defence area to make it clear that it was a
friendly aircraft. Bristol couldn't answer these questions. So I cabled Bermuda as each need became
known. For a time Bermuda officialdom was reluctant

to disclose these secrets to an organisation branch - our signal prefix had indicated that that was what we were. And we were in doubt whether the small administration which my messages were reaching knew anything about the operation anyway. So I sought out a senior on the Air Staff, who cabled the highest level he could reach, requesting that my messages be immediately answered and co-operation be given.

As the morning advanced, word got around the Air Ministry and other Ministries that a VIP flight was in progress. Then our phone became busy with enquiries to the point we had to move to another office to get our messages out. Fighter Command wished to have the flying-boat escorted; Coastal Command wanted to give it long range cover; the radar organisation had queries; the protocol people wanted to know where to place their experts to receive and coddle the passengers. More and more people got in on the act, and we never knew who should and who should not. If Berlin had phoned us, sounding convincing, I doubt if we could have sorted them out from the rest. Altogether, it was an organisational shambles. And no one could make out why an organisation branch, located in Bush House, Aldwych, was dealing direct with an important aircraft with a VIP on board.

A squadron of fighters was directed out to escort the flying-boat. The first message over the radio from the flying-boat was a call in the clear from its Captain: 'I am being attacked by fighters.' The Captain was only too aware that just a few months earlier a BOAC Liberator with a VIP passenger list approaching Cornwall was accidentally shot down by Polish fighters. Fighter Control then reported that its squadron commander had seen the flying-boat dive to sea-level and begin to jink about. So they withdrew the fighter escort to a discreet distance.

There was yet another scare, which went the rounds of the 'rumour factory'. Each day the Germans sent out a meteorological flight from Brittany to the West of Ireland. Radar observers in the UK reported that the blip of the German plane had merged with the blip of the flying-boat on their screens. This could have meant an interception. I very much doubted whether a German weather plane, flying at a very different level, would have spotted the flying-boat. If it had done so, it would have avoided attack, since flying-boats were reckoned to have a heavy sting in their tails. Also, at several hundred miles away, a radar blip covered a big area of air. The planes could have been miles apart. However, all over town the story went round that Winston Churchill had nearly been shot down.

A day or two later, Chief of the Air Staff Sir Charles Portal held a post mortem on this flight with his Air Staff Air Marshals. He must have learnt that there was no air staff who dealt with air transport or special flights, but only a Wing Commander in Organisation. So I was summoned to Whitehall and the Air Staff side of the Air Ministry to be taken into the Chief's presence by the Air Marshal who had helped me open up Bermuda to release those radio secrets. The VIP, he told me, had been delighted by the flight, especially its speed, since it had taken less than twenty-four

hours to make the trip which had taken him a week
by battleship. Now he wanted to visit the Middle East
and Teheran in Persia (Iran).

Sir Charles ruled that in future the RAF must carry
VIPs, particularly when they pass through a war zone
- which of course included all of Britain. He instructed
me to find a suitable aircraft to convey the VIP to the
new destinations. I only knew of one aircraft in the
RAF which could fly these distances and also be
suitable for passengers. This was a Liberator I which
the A.O.C. Ferry Command, in Montreal, used for his
visits to American aircraft factories. The A.O.C. was
the most senior Air Chief Marshal in the RAF, Sir
Frederick Bowhill, who would have retired, had it not
been for the war.

A few days before my summons to Sir Charles Portal
I had seen a copy of a personal signal to Sir Frederick
from the Vice-Chief of the Air Staff, Sir Wilfred
Freeman. Sir Wilfred had a suspicion that Sir Frederick
had diverted a Liberator bomber, due for delivery to
the UK and had had it fitted out to a civilian standard
as a communications aircraft for his visits in America.
So Sir Wilfred's signal enquired, 'Where is Liberator
AL 504?' A reply came saying that AL 504 was in
Montreal and unserviceable. A second signal from Sir
Wilfred enquired when it would be serviceable for
delivery. I had watched this cannonade between the
big shots and knew that Sir Frederick was on the spot.

It was just at this time that I received the instruction
from Sir Charles Portal to produce a suitable VIP
aircraft, so I had great joy in speeding my signal to Sir

Frederick asking for a suitably equipped aircraft with the best crew to fly a VIP overseas. Within hours I received a signal that AL 504 was airborne for Northolt, outside London, naming the crew. I asked Dismore, our expert, to give me a run-down on these men. The first pilot, Captain Van der Kloot, second pilot Captain Ruggles and three other members of the crew were all American citizens, non-combatants. I was told that they wore smart dark blue uniforms with rank stripes on the arms.

I next phoned my contacts in the Personnel branches to ask them if they could produce within twenty-four hours an RAF crew qualified and experienced to fly a Liberator I. I knew that such a crew did not exist, except possibly in the Liberator conversion unit at Bermuda. My aim was to alert my friends to the call I guessed would come from the highest level in due course. Then I went to Whitehall to see Sir Charles Portal about the crew for the VIP flight. When I told him about the American crewmen, he picked up the phone and called the Air Member for Personnel, asking for an experienced RAF Liberator crew right away. A reply soon came back stating that such a crew did not exist on this side of the Atlantic. Then I made a proposal - could we not insert into this civilian crew an RAF navigator who would provide the Service link? Sir Charles thought this was a good idea and phoned the AMP 'to arrange the best navigator available for this special flight.'

Meanwhile Van der Kloot and his crew had moved into the Savoy Hotel in London and I went to see them there. I said to Van der Kloot, 'I notice you don't have a navigator in your crew.' He replied, 'I do the navigating.' I broke it to him that the RAF wished to put a navigator aboard his plane for this special flight, and pointed out how useful a liaison officer would be to him at the stations they would be visiting. 'Fine,' said Van der Kloot, 'provided he doesn't interfere with the navigation of my ship.' In the event, it worked out well; the chosen squadron leader was something of a diplomat and made himself wholly accepted by the crew.

Late one evening, Sir Charles took me to No. 10 Downing Street, the Prime Minister's official residence. It was pitch dark and everything was so secret that I had no idea where I was or who I should meet, or even who were to be the passengers on this special flight. Van der Kloot and Ruggles were escorted there separately. As we waited in an anteroom I had the feeling I had been in the room before. Then I realised I'd seen a film about the younger Pitt, Prime Minister during the Napoleonic War. The film set must have been modelled on this room.

Sir Charles and I were ushered into a long room with an oval table in the middle. Seated around the table were the Chiefs of Staff and top civil servants, many of whom I recognised from newspaper photographs. In the middle was seated Winston Churchill, the Prime Minister, dressed in a blue siren suit, a one piece affair. I heard him say, 'Who is this young man?' Portal replied, 'He is your air transport adviser, sir.' This was the first time I had heard myself so described. Churchill waved me to a seat opposite him. As I reached it, he said, 'Meet my First Sea Lord.' I looked down at the Admiral, and it seemed as though the gold stripes on his arm went right up his sleeve to mingle with the rows of medals on his chest. He was Admiral Sir Dudley Pound. He looked terribly ill to me, and soon afterwards he died.

The Prime Minister looked at me and said, 'So you are taking me to see Joe?' For a wild moment I couldn't think who on earth Joe might be. Then I realised it was Joseph Stalin. I replied, 'Yes, sir.' 'Well, what will it be like in Teheran? Will I need warm underclothing?' I made a quick guess and boldly offered my opinion. Then we broke the news that we had an excellent aircraft, with the best crew Ferry Command could produce, but they were all Americans and non-combatants. Of course there would be an RAF officer with them. The Prime Minister responded, 'Well, I'm half American. Bring them in.'

When our two pilots appeared in the doorway, their faces were a study as they became aware of whom it was they were meeting. The Prime Minister was wonderful with them, inviting them to take chairs on either side of him, asking them about their homes and their families. Then he asked, 'Can you take me to Teheran safely?' Van der Kloot replied, 'We will take you anywhere you want to go, if the aircraft can reach it.'

A day or two later, while we were excessively busy trying to clear up the paper work of the special flight and get the flow of reinforcements stepped up and everything back to normal, two gentlemen presented themselves in my tiny office. They explained they were from the Cabinet Office Security and wished to

ask a few questions about the special flight operation.
'Did you know,' they asked, 'that German radio
announced that the Prime Minister and party had
flown from Britain to Gibraltar en route to the Middle
East to see Stalin?' I did not. Naturally they had to
enquire how this information might have reached the
Germans. I and my secretary, a lady temporary civil
servant, were two sources they had to investigate.

They stayed around the office for three days, totally
disrupting our work and blocking the mass of telephone calls from our units required to continue our
flying operations. Time and again they asked the
question, 'Why did you do that?' to the most routine
of actions. 'Why did you speak to RAF station X on an
open line, rather than on a scrambler line?' (Answer:
neither I nor the station had a scrambler.) I frequently
made the point that all these messages to and fro were
routine, and if one did not know a VIP was involved,
were absolutely normal communications. They wrote
it all down. It was a distressing experience, not least
because my excellent secretary offered her resignation:
'As they do not trust me.'

Over the next two years the Prime Minister and his
advisers made a number of special flights to the
Mediterranean, Cairo, Casablanca, Moscow and Yalta,
on the Black Sea. Each of them required a break away
from all other duties and total devotion to each
operation, usually for several weeks ahead and until
the VIPs returned. Yet, all the time, the flow of
reinforcements and ferry flights was increasing. We
also had a growing load of Organisational work to do,
planning, creating units, and later on, squadrons.

Apart from our four specialists on the North Atlantic ferry crews, our office staff never exceeded seven. We were working six and seven days a week, from morning until late at night - and occasionally all night, when a special flight was in progress.

These flights required the selection of aircraft and crew, alerting and instructing the stations along the route and the wireless controls, and all the arrangements within the Air Ministry. Often there were special features like planning with the Security branches to keep operations secret and to divert attention. On top of that, there was liaison with the Foreign Office when foreign governments were involved, to keep them instructed on the flying and control arrangements and other matters.

I much enjoyed cooking up with Security plans to mislead the curious when a VIP flight was scheduled. Once, when the Prime Minister wished to fly to the Middle East, a story was leaked in Parliament and certain clubs (and need I add that it was all around town in no time) that the Prime Minister was off to see President Roosevelt in the USA.

A day or two before the flight, a security officer phoned me, 'Guess what has just been reported to me,' he said. 'A small van with the name of a famous men's outfitter on its side has just driven up to No. 10 (the Prime Minister's office and home), where the public can see everything, and a little man has opened the van's back doors, piled up a stack of pith helmets up to his chin and staggered into the house. Bang goes our cover story of his visiting the frozen wastes of North America!'

I recall another occasion when we were sending the Prime Minister overseas from an Oxfordshire airfield. For three days prior to the event a security cordon had been thrown around the area, all mail delayed, telephones put out of order, posters displayed stressing the need for security. When the flight was away, a security post mortem was held. One security officer produced a postcard, mailed in the box outside the Station Guard Room, and read it aloud: 'Dear Mum, Guess who I saw off in an aircraft tonight? Winston Ch...ll.'

Yet again, when a security guard was walking around the Liberator while it awaited its distinguished passenger and party, he looked into the front bomb aimer's window. Inside he saw a fine pile of suitcases, each of which was clearly labelled, 'The Prime Minister, Moscow.'

One day I received word that King George VI was to be flown to North Africa to visit his armies. More than ever before my every action was supervised by people who had no idea of the operational problems to be solved. Again and again my efforts to keep the flying operation as routine as possible were over-ruled. I took the view that if the normal cyphers were used for our routine messages no suspicions would be aroused in the German Y listening service, who monitored all our wireless messages. Immediately an unusual cypher was used through our regular radio station they would begin to take an interest in why, and whether that flight was of unusual interest. My view was supported by the working officers who handled our traffic and who listened to the German traffic. I recognised the fear some senior officers might feel that if anything went wrong they would be criticised for not applying extra security. So the increase in wireless traffic, the unusual cyphers, the positioning of naval vessels along the route could have indicated to the German Y service, if they were alert, that a VIP flight would be crossing the Bay of Biscay, within range. However, the Germans showed no obvious response when the flight departed, so our fears were probably unwarranted.

The hot blasts down my neck from a multitude of top brass during the week of preparation were very stressful, as we worked at our peak. Each one thought his subject was the most important for my attention. By comparison, the flight itself, in a York, went without a hitch. The basic problem was that a VIP flight was under the direct control of a Wing Commander in an Air Ministry office, rather than under the direction of an operating Group or Station, where a senior officer, whose competence was recognised, would be in sole charge.

Once the flight was on its way I sat up all night in my office, waiting. I knew there was nothing I could do to alter anything, but I also knew that my top brass might phone at any time to enquire how the operation was going, just as though we had an operations room manned twenty-four hours a day. Sure enough, at about 3 a.m. the telephone rang. 'Portal here,' said a voice. 'Foss, what would you do if this special flight came down in the sea?' I thought fast and replied, 'I would originate a Casualty Signal, sir.' 'Well, you never know,' said the Chief of Air Staff, 'You had better consider what you would say.' I set about drafting a message about an accident that had not happened and whose details were just a guess. I realised that, apart from the crew and the King, I had only a vague idea who was aboard the aircraft. It reminded me of a newspaper crossword puzzle which, to ensure winning a prize, required hundreds of permutations submitted. I suspected that CAS was also sitting in his office wondering and feeling he needed to reassure himself to break the monotony.

As the King's York approached Gibraltar, a patch of fog rolled off the sea and over the runway, which stuck out like a pier into the harbour. It was barely a hundred yards from the Spanish frontier, where guards could not be guaranteed to hold their fire if an aircraft strayed too close. A local aircraft might find its way in under those conditions, but it was out of the question to land the King's aircraft. The Flying Control had to divert. The only RAF station within the York's range was Ras el Mar, a bulldozed strip and tented camp near Fez in Morocco. We used Ras el Mar when we sent reinforcement aircraft from Britain to the Algiers-based RAF Command. There were also American bases in the area, but they had not been warned of the flight.

So the York was headed to Ras. Its last message heard in UK was a 'reeling in', as the operator wound in his aerial before the landing. Unlike today, with voice transmissions carried with great clarity over long distances, communication then was by Morse between a wireless operator on board and another on the ground.

We had notified Ras the day before that there would be no aircraft from UK that night. When the York circled Ras, we learnt later, the duty flying control corporal hurried to the control. The Captain of the aircraft called on his radio telephone and said, 'Inform your Commanding Officer at once that we have a VIP aboard.' The corporal was not sufficiently confident to awake his CO on the strength of a radio message, so he leapt on his bicycle and hurried to the aircraft to confirm who was aboard. Then he dashed a mile to the camp and the tent where his CO was asleep. The corporal shook him awake, shouting, 'Sir, the King is on the airfield.' 'You're crazy,' said the Wing Commander. 'No, sir, cross my heart and prepare to die, it is the King.' The Wing Commander jumped from his bed and pulled on his clothes. Then he felt his chin, and decided that he could not greet His Majesty unshaven. He set about shaving and in his agitation cut himself. Dabbing his cut, he pulled on his tunic and rushed to the airfield.

Meanwhile, on the airfield a Dakota had just landed, bringing a new Wing Commander, who was to take over command. This officer hurried over to where the King and his entourage were discussing what they should do. He did his best to make them welcome. The King, probably to make conversation, asked him, 'Have you been here long?' 'About twenty minutes, sir.' His Majesty must have gained an unusual impression of how we ran the Royal Air Force.

I had to 'do business' with Sir Charles Portal over each of these high level flights, and I developed a very great respect for the Chief of the Air Staff. The flights had both political and international ramifications, explosive if anything went wrong. Although I was a very young Wing Commander, Sir Charles always treated me as though I were one of his Air Vice-Marshals in charge of a branch of the Air Staff - the policy makers. He asked my opinion and he listened. Then he gave a ruling and, if necessary, an explanation of the factors that brought him to that decision. I knew where I stood, what was expected and what authority I needed. Then he would leave me to get on with the job.

One day I received instructions from the CAS's office about a special flight from the UK to Egypt via Gibraltar on which Portal was to travel. On the leg from Gibraltar to Cairo the aircraft was to report its position each hour. I was sure that this would increase the hazards of the flight and was unnecessary. How could I get the order reversed? I phoned Portal's Staff Officer and asked if I might see CAS. The reply came back, 'Only if it is a matter of life and death; he is so busy preparing for the flight.' I swallowed and said, 'It is a matter of life and death.' Portal would see me. I took along two security officers. I laid on his desk a map on which I had marked the probable track from Gibraltar to Egypt and along it I had marked the hourly points where the aircraft would be reported - ten times in a twelve hour flight. I had also marked the estimated positions of German fighters based in the desert and close to the track.

I explained my marks on the map. 'Sir,' I said, 'an aircraft that reports every hour becomes of interest to the German Y wireless. By the tenth transmission they will have fixed its track and will have sent up a fighter to investigate and intercept - about here.' And I put my finger on the map. Portal looked up at me and said, 'You are asking me to change my mind?' 'Yes, sir.' 'Very well, I change my mind.' He added, 'And who are these two officers?' I introduced them and explained that they would confirm that the German fighters were probably at the estimated point. 'Thank you, gentlemen, for coming,' he said, as we withdrew.

Mine was very much of a chauffeur's view of VIPs. Some were marvellous in appreciating our difficulties, thinking ahead and telling us what they expected. They did what we asked them to do and showed trust in our judgement. King George VI was certainly the best example. But there were others! One well-known Secretary of State refused to board a twin-engined aircraft because he felt his position warranted a four-engined plane. The airfield to which he wanted us to fly him was too small for a four-engined aircraft to land safely. After high words, he left by road. Another VIP arrived at the departure field hours late for a flight which crossed the Bay of Biscay. His tardiness meant that he was asking us to fly him in daylight within interception distance of German bases, which we could not permit. To complicate matters, he had brought several lady officials who were unsuitably dressed for the rough and ready and very cold bomb bay of our Liberator. He then complained that he had not been informed of the unsuitable aircraft the RAF was providing.

By far the most complex and anxiety-provoking flights I had to arrange were those into Russia. On the first such flight, and most of the others, the Prime Minister and many important personages were our passengers. The Russians in London could tell us nothing in advance of the safest route to fly, nor even the location of the airfield of arrival or of what diversions to make if the weather closed in. Information about their wireless facilities, navigational aids and direction-finding seemed to be too secret to lever out of Moscow officialdom. Unlike every other country in the world, they did not recognise the International Q code, which made possible the exchange of navigational messages in any language when using Morse.

So, before each flight we had to agree the code and the meaning for each item. It was a laborious business, because it all had to be cyphered and sent by diplomatic wireless to the British Embassy in Moscow, who in turn had to decipher it and then reconcile it with their counterparts in Moscow, who were not necessarily aviators. Our messages choked the Embassy's lines at a time when their other diplomatic messages were at a peak, preparing for a high level international conference. Our messages had to be prefixed 'O' for Organisation, and that sometimes pushed them down in importance, just when flying operations needed the highest priority.

After our first flight into Russia their authorities insisted that we make a landing on their border to permit a Russian wireless operator aboard. He took over our wireless sets and used them to report to the ground as the flight proceeded. Never once did he

give any navigational aid to the aircrew, while effec-
tively denying them any way to help themselves. The
Prime Minister told me once, with a certain pride, that
he always had a Russian aboard when he flew to
Moscow; he did not understand how much more
hazardous that made the flight.

On an early flight to Moscow our pilot was much
shaken when a Russian fighter escorting him suddenly
fired his front guns across his nose. It was the only
way the fighter knew to point to an airfield where he
required our plane to land. There was another occasion, with the Prime Minister aboard, when our pilot,
flying in the heavy murk in the vicinity of Moscow,
glimpsed an airfield on which he supposed he was to
land. He made to land and was almost at touchdown
when a passenger came forward to tell him that a mile
or two away he had seen an airfield with lines of
troops and other signs of a reception. So the pilot
opened up and flew round to find this other, and
correct, airfield.

On yet another occasion the weather came right
down and our pilot was forced to land on a military
airfield nearby. The crew were shocked when they
were put to sleep in a large barracks room whose other
occupants were both airmen and airwomen. However,
they were relieved that it was so cold that everyone
slept in all their clothes.

As the war continued, these special flights became
more frequent and involved larger numbers of passengers and more complex organisation. The largest operation was the movement to Yalta for the conference
which parcelled out conquered Europe between East

and West. To mount that operation we had to transport close to 600 men to man the airfields, controls and wireless. Fortunately by that time we had a big organisation to handle it. Our small office in Organisation, Air Ministry, had been replaced by an Air Staff branch in Whitehall and a full Headquarters of RAF Transport Command.

8

Action with Allies

My duties in the Air Ministry were frequently enlive-
ned by contacts with the citizens of other countries,
some of them amusing, some invigorating and some
infuriating. It was first vividly borne in on me that we
had friends and allies in the war when I was on the
troopship carrying me back from the Middle East in
1941. There I met Polish and Czech officers, mainly
fellow pilots. They had horrific stories to tell of the
invasion of their countries by both Germans and
Russians. They told of their hardships and starvation
as they walked and travelled, many of them for
months, to get away from prison camps to join us in
the fight. Finally when they had made their way to
Palestine, they had been thrust into POW camps. That
was the hardest to bear, since they wondered whether
they would ever be allowed to fight for their country
with their allies. Some of them I met again later in the
war.

Very different were my contacts with some other
allies soon after starting my ferrying work in the Air
Ministry. I approached the Russian Embassy for information about Murmansk when I had to plan for the

fighter squadrons we were to send there and I encountered a wall of suspicion from its officers. I
realised that Russia had only recently been our enemy,
as she joined with the Germans in attacking our allies,
the Poles, as well as gallant Finland. Probably their few
officers sent over to form an embassy military staff felt
lost and insecure. We certainly became very suspicious
of them and their stone-walling tactics.

Then came the first special flight to Teheran for
Churchill to meet Stalin. I realised that we had to build
a relationship with individuals at the Embassy in order
for them to advise us and transmit such of our plans
as we felt they must know.

I became more deeply involved with the Russians
around that same time, when the United States entered the war. The Americans offered Russia some 100
DC3 transport planes. The Russian Ambassador was
soon around to call on the Foreign Secretary, Anthony
Eden, suggesting that Britain should be equally gener-
ous to Russia, now the only country fighting the
Germans, and exhausting them. So the Air Ministry
offered 100 of a new bomber, the Albemarle, now being
mass-produced. At that time it seemed that in RAF
operations there was no role for this bomber. I entered
the picture when I was told to prepare with the
Russian military for the training of their pilots and
crews, so that they could take delivery of these aircraft
and fly them to Russia.

After several secretive phone calls, a posse of Russian officers arrived in my office. We made them tea
and they passed the time of day, talking through their
interpreter. They asked general questions about the

war, the weather and other matters about which they could have learned as much from the newspapers as from me. After a 'happy' two hours they suddenly rose to leave. At that point their leader - I understood him to be a General - asked one question which revealed their real reason for the visit: 'What do you think of the Albemarle?' I had never heard of the Albemarle until instructions reached me from above. I only knew that it was a twin-engined bomber, probably originally intended for daylight operations, in the same class as the Blenheim. Its performance, like all other details, was shrouded in secrecy. I told the General I would be able to tell him more on his next visit, which he paid a couple of weeks later.

I was working under great pressure and felt I could not afford to spend another couple of hours on 'happy' talk before we reached key questions. I was also clear that this delegation could only refer information to Moscow for an answer or agreement, and that looked like a long process. I was also sure that the General could understand English, even though everything had to go through his interpreter. So for the next visit I wrote a short memo, giving all the facts I had and also the proposal we were making, particularly for the training of his ferry crews.

This time, only the General, an officer and the interpreter arrived, settled themselves down and began the general conversation again. I let them have a few minutes and then gave them my memo to read. There was much talk between them about it. They seemed to be treating it as though it were an international treaty drawn up between lawyers, instead of something I had dictated to my secretary with no thought of legal implications. Then the General proclaimed through his interpreter, 'This is excellent. It answers all our questions - all except one.' 'And what is that?' 'You do not give the date for the operation to commence.' I suggested, 'You choose the date.' It was now September.

They studied their diaries and after a warm discussion, the General announced, 'We shall start on the twenty-fifth of December.' Unthinking, I replied, 'Oh, no, we can't start on that date.' At once the General replied very heatedly, in English, 'And why not?' I explained that December 25th was a very special date for us, but we would be delighted to start on the 26th. The interpreter went into a lengthy discourse, probably explaining the significance of Christmas. The General rose to his feet, took my hand and wrung it, as the interpreter explained that the General wished us all a merry Christmas. Then they went.

We set about at once preparing for the Russian ferry pilots to come, although I was sure we would see none of them before Christmas, and certainly their training would take a month or two. It was nearly a year before the first Russian crews arrived. In conjunction with the appropriate branches I chose a training airfield on the east coast of Scotland, as this would permit the Russian crews to take off direct for Russia when they were ready. When they did arrive we hit several unexpected snags. The pilots selected to train them had to speak Russian, so we picked Czechs, not realising their hatred for the Russians because of the treatment they had received in their camps before escaping to Palestine. We were able to overcome that bitterness. But that was only the start of our troubles.

The Russian Ambassador insisted that there be a direct telephone line from the station to his embassy. So every minor complaint caused him to reach for his top hat and march to the Foreign Office, who took it all very seriously, and I had to drop whatever I was doing and investigate and report back. Then the Russian crews insisted that they have unlimited whisky, at a time when for everyone else it was in very short supply. The Station Commander suggested to me that a pipeline be installed from the nearest distillery, as the demand was exceeding his transport facilities!

A much more serious problem arose when we found that inadvertently we had placed the Russians right in the middle of the area of Scotland being defended by the Polish Division. Once the Poles got word that their hated Russians were in the RAF camp there was such a commotion we seriously considered calling in a battalion of British troops to guard the station. The Army was able to deal with the issue, but we in the RAF were embarrassed at not having foreseen the problem.

When the Russian crews were being sorted out upon arrival, one group of four was asked which was the pilot, the navigator, the wireless operator and the gunner. The little man leading the group responded, 'I am a Hero of the Soviet Union. I can bring who I like.' This included at least two of them who had no qualifications whatever for the tasks. Then we discovered something else about a Hero. He did not

expect to pay for things in shops; a grateful country
gave them to him. But the local Scottish shopkeepers
had not heard of this privilege, and arrests were made
for shoplifting. These swiftly stirred the Ambassador
to tackle the Foreign Office.

One day I received an invitation to attend the
celebration of Red Army Day at the Russian Embassy.
I went along at the time printed on my invitation, to
find almost no other guests and tables still being set
up and food being laid out. I was offered a cup of tea
and gratefully retired with it behind a pillar to watch
the scene in the big hall, dotted with fine statues.
Eventually preparations were completed and people
began to arrive. Most seemed aware that the know-
ledgeable arrived an hour after the advertised time at
a Russian 'do'.

Soon the hall was packed with service people and
civilians and through the crowd slid waiters holding
above their heads glasses of vodka. I hung on to my
cup of tea. Then, in the midst of the crowd appeared
a V of tough-looking civilians, and behind them my
General. These men roughly pushed aside everyone
as they marched in the direction the General indicated.
Suddenly he saw me and in moments the way had
been cleared to bring us face to face. 'You have no
vodka,' said the General. 'Vodka, vodka!' he shouted.
Waiters converged from all directions. 'No, no, thank
you,' I said, 'I am very happy with my tea.' 'What!'
cried the General fiercely, 'You will not drink to the
Red Army?' I prayed for help and it came. I said,
'General, you see, I feel it here,' putting my hand on
my heart, 'not here,' and held my stomach. There was

a pause, and everyone watched the General. Suddenly he burst out laughing, slapped me on the shoulder and turned away, pointing a new direction to his toughs. I watched him advancing around the hall, gesticulating to people, holding his heart and his stomach and laughing his head off. And of course the toughs roared too, though they probably didn't understand a word I'd said. The rule seemed to be: when a General laughs, everybody laughs.

I joined some RAF Equipment colleagues and we moved into a side room to raid the snacks table. There we ran into some English-speaking Russian officers, who seemed to know we were involved with the gift of Albemarles. They said, 'Those planes are no good, you know. Why cannot we have transport planes like the US Dakotas?' I explained that we just did not have them, and we were giving the best that we had. I added that if nothing else was of use to them, the excellent Bristol engines, two per plane, would be, and after all, this was a gift from one hard-pressed nation to another. At that, one Russian said, 'Those nice navigator watches I have seen, with stop action and all else - we might persuade our people to take the Albemarles if we had watches like that.' I asked the Equipment people if that could be arranged. 'One for each of us,' the Russian quickly added. My colleagues said they felt sure that it could be arranged and took the names of the Russian officers. So, for the price of six navigator watches, the Albemarles were accepted. But only twelve were ever collected.

Later, when it was clear that the Russians were unhappy about the Albemarles, higher authority agreed to supply Mosquitoes, another light bomber. The Russian ferry pilots were taken to a nearby RAF station to see the plane and the equipment. Almost at once the Ambassador was at the Foreign Office, complaining that we were again fobbing off our old equipment on them. The ferry pilots had complained that the Mosquitoes they were to receive were Mark V. The Mosquitoes they had seen at the RAF station were Mark XXV. Answer, Mark V was a bomber, Mark XXV was a specialised photo reconnaissance aircraft.

I went to have a quiet talk with the officer responsible for issuing orders to the stores depot to release aircraft. He explained to me what the difference was between the models. We agreed that he would arrange for the Russians' Mosquitoes to be numbered XXXV. This made the Russians very happy. Almost every week hiccups like this occurred to keep the Ambassador, the Russian Desk at the Foreign Office, and my office well occupied.

Almost three years later, the General visited me without his interpreter. We conversed in English and finally he came around to a favour he wished to ask me. I was able to grant it. We could not have been more friendly. Soon afterwards he returned to Russia.

Another ally who kept me busy were the Americans. In 1942 the occasional American began coming to my office, particularly a Colonel from the US Embassy. He was responsible for overseeing the preparations for the US Army Air Force to fly in to Britain. We quickly became good friends. I shall never forget the steak I ate in his mess -as much good meat as I normally had in a fortnight, in one piece on my plate. Soon after that, I had a message from the Secretary of State, Sir Archibald Sinclair, instructing me to inform him immediately I heard that the US Air Force was due to arrive, as he wished to be at Prestwick to meet them and make them welcome.

I asked my Colonel friend to find out for me when they were due. For months he kept telling me that he was trying, but could get no straight answer out of the Commanding General of the First US Air Force in Maine. Finally he showed me a cable, 'Personal from Hunter, Commanding General. I am entrusted by the President to bring my Air Force safely to Britain. When I do, and where, is my responsibility and I will inform you when I choose.'

One day the Group Captain commanding at Prestwick rang me up. 'You asked me to let you know when the US Air Force arrives,' he said. 'Well, I can see it from my office. It is one transport plane with US markings - not a civilian transport such as we've been getting every few days - and it's moving down to the end of the runway. I'm going out to see what it's all about.' I rang the Secretary of State's office and told them what I'd heard. They were not interested.

Then the Group Captain phoned again. 'When I got to the US transport, it had parked near the top end of the runway. There was a lieutenant in charge. Two of his men were digging a hole beyond the end of the runway. I asked them what they were doing and the Lieutenant produced an Order directing him to erect a radio station for homing purposes. I pointed to the forest of masts upwind of the runway and asked him what he thought that was for. He said he had his orders and would go on. I drove back to the Guard-room and picked up two RAF policemen with a Sten gun and a clip of ammunition.

Then I drove to the US transport, where the men had got down shoulder high in their hole. I said to the officer, 'Listen to what I say to the policeman.: "Load your gun, now stand by that hole. If anyone, but anyone, tries to get into the hole you are to shoot him dead." I said to the officer, 'Did you hear what my orders were?' 'Yes,' said the officer. I asked him, 'What are you going to do now?' 'I will fly back to the States and ask for further orders.' After refuelling, he took off. Shortly afterwards, the bombers of First Air Force, followed by the Eighth Air Force, arrived in big groups, not only at Prestwick, but at airfields all over the country.

One early visitor to my office was a Major, who produced a questionnaire and asked me a lot of questions, thanked me and left. About six weeks later another officer arrived, pulled out the same question-naire and asked the same questions. I resented the time this took and told him so. He told me that on his return flight, the Major had to make a forced landing on the central massif in Greenland. They were still trying to rescue him.

Once we got to know one another and our ways, we got on well, and I found the Americans very helpful to us time and again. In Iceland, for instance, when we asked the Treasury for an establishment for a staging post there, we were granted one officer and 25 men. The equivalent unit for the USAAF was nearly

1200. In summer Iceland has nearly twenty-four hours of daylight and in no time our men were sick with overwork. The US offered to take over our duties, and did so. Similarly, in Bahrain, in the Gulf, the American air-conditioned quarters (built by British reverse lend-lease) were a haven for our overworked men, who lived in palm leaf huts under ghastly hot and humid conditions.

There were some amusing differences between the American and Russian approach to issues. In contrast to the endless red tape of the Russians, I found the Americans at times remarkably casual, even in government matters. A memorable example occurred one Saturday morning as I cleared my desk at the end of a busy week, hoping to get everything finished so that I would not have to work on Sunday.

My chief had a tendency to put difficult files in a separate tray, where they lay until Friday afternoon, when he would mark them out to be dealt with by different members of his staff. One Saturday morning I found such a file on my desk. It contained a request from our American allies to build an airfield on Ascension Island. All I vaguely knew about the island was that it was in the South Atlantic and not very large. I decided to phone around. I called the Foreign Office. They said, 'Try the Colonial office.' The Colonial Office said, 'Try Cable and Wireless - they own the island.' I rang Cable and Wireless, but they said the man who knew all about Ascension Island was away for the weekend. 'We'll get him to send you something on Monday.' I said that was too late. I had to send a reply to Washington that day.

I phoned the Admiralty and they sent me a large-scale chart, which was very useful, because I was able to go over it with protractors and find where it might be possible to put a runway on the island. I rang the Civil Aviation Department, located in Bristol and they said they would send plans for an airport which they had prepared a few years before. These arrived two weeks later. The only idea I had left was to ring the library of the Air Ministry. A lady there said the best work they had on Ascension Island was the *Encyclopaedia Britannica* (which was published in America!) She sent a messenger over with the relevant volume. In it I found several important items; there was only sufficient water on the island to supply the Cable and Wireless personnel there; at certain times of the year it was impossible to land because of the very heavy surf, and there was a difficulty with the birds, which used it intensively as a nesting place.

So I prepared a cable for my chief to send - in fact, I sent it on his behalf. In it we agreed to the Americans building a runway on Ascension Island, but its owners were the Cable and Wireless Company, and it remained British territory. I added information about the difficulties of water shortage, surf and birds. As soon as the cable went off I got on with the next job and never thought about it again.

About eighteen months later, an American gentleman came through my office door and asked if I was Foss. When I told him I was, he laid on my desk a series of large photographs of a runway, with mountains on either side of it. That, he said, was Ascension Island. I asked if they'd had any difficulties in building it. Yes, he said, they'd taken notice of the fact that they'd have to build a pier, make provision for water, but the real difficulty they had was with the birds. They were still trying to find a way to keep them off the runway.

In 1982, during the Falkland Islands war, Ascension Island was crucial as a refuelling stop for the British aircraft. I read that the birds were still a problem.

One of the few serious disagreements I had with Americans came over language. I realised that we did not always speak the same one. Once traffic across the Atlantic began to be heavy, an issue arose which required urgent solution. The RAF Controller was signalling 'stop', while the US Controller signalled 'come on', like two rival point duty policemen. An American Colonel came to see me and we agreed to confer and come up with a combined flying control agreement. We worked on it for a fortnight, between other duties. The big snag proved to be that when I said, 'The Controller will do ... ' the RAF had one understanding and the US quite another. Time and again he said, 'You cannot say it like that. I could never obtain a conviction in a Court Martial with that language.'

One day, I said to him, 'I recommend that I have my control instructions translated into French and you do likewise. Then we get a Frenchman to agree on a text and we work from that.' 'But I can't speak French,' he said. 'Nor can I,' I replied, 'but I don't see how we can agree on language any other way!' In the end, we agreed to couch our control instructions each in our own way, and then make an agreement that we would co-ordinate and work in that spirit. Those flying regulations lasted for years.

Soon after the Colonel and I had come to terms, however, trouble broke out in another quarter. I was summoned to the office of my ultimate chief, Sir Christopher Courtenay, a member of the Air Council. He showed me a signal from the Air Marshal who headed the RAF delegation in Washington. It read: 'Who is Foss? By what authority does he agree flying control regulations with the USAAF?' The message went on to enquire what we thought was the purpose of a delegation in Washington, if not for such matters.

Just as Sir Christopher was getting into it, a call came saying that the Secretary of State wished to see me and my chief, Air Vice-Marshal Hollinghurst, about this matter. So it now entered the realm of the political. Over to Whitehall 'Holly' and I went. We stood outside the Secretary of State's office like a couple of school-boys waiting to see the Headmaster. Finally, we were ushered in and the file was laid in front of Sir Archibald. At that moment a summons came for him to see the Prime Minister. As he leapt up to go, Sir Archibald said, 'This must be dealt with by the Under-Secretary' (Captain Harold Balfour).

So out we went to wait for the Captain. When we went in, Balfour was leafing through the file, obviously trying to see what the matter was. He opened by saying, 'Air Vice-Marshal, this is a serious matter. What have you to say?' Holly replied, 'I have a big depart-ment and I have to leave things to my officers. Foss knows the facts and I think he should answer.' I said,

'Sir, I think when you have read the file, you will agree that we did what was in the best interests of the RAF' Balfour looked nonplussed and hesitated. Then he said, 'Well, it is a grave matter and it shouldn't happen again.' And we were dismissed. As we walked down the long passage outside, Holly looked up and down it and then hissed into my ear, 'I hate politicians.'

One final reminiscence about encounters with Americans. In 1943, after the Allies had made their landings in North Africa, I was sent post haste to Algiers. In Algiers I met the Air Officer Commanding our Transport Group (No 216) in Cairo, Air Commodore Whitney Straight, who had been a noted golfer, road racer and aircraft manufacturer and was born of American parents. We had to sort out with the American air transport General, who was a noted civil airline operator, which facilities at the big French airfield of Maison Blanche, Algiers, should go to the RAF and which to the USAAF.

North Africa was an American War zone and the General was a go-getter. But Straight was his match. A plan of the airfield was laid out before us and Straight said, 'This is the hangar we have earmarked for you, General,' pointing to the hangar at the end of the row. The General stared over Straight's shoulder and finally remarked, 'What, that ventilated hangar?' When I went out to the airfield I saw the hangar. It had had a bomb explode in the middle of it and it looked like an enormous colander. I must add that our own hangar was little better.

Relations with the Frenchmen I met during the war tended to be complicated. After the collapse of France in 1940, General De Gaulle and other French officers arrived in Britain. Attempts were made to create a Free French Air Force and other forces. Difficulties arose because our Government did not know whom to trust and build on. There were protagonists for each of the different elements among the escapees, and we received many subterranean messages from Vichy and other occupied areas of the French empire which blackguarded one group of French or another. The French officers themselves seemed unable to agree. Our Government was reluctant to allow them into the planning side of the war in case they were spies or turncoats. It was all very complicated, and rebounded into our office, because it was our duty to provide new aircraft to whichever Force was in favour at that moment.

One day I was talking to a Free French Air Force Colonel. He complained, 'Those Wellingtons you have provided us with, they are lovely aircraft. We so much enjoy flying them. But each of them has rubber strings.' 'Rubber strings?' I asked. 'Yes, we fly them for a few weeks and are really beginning to enjoy them and planning to go over and bomb the Hun. Then suddenly they are snatched away by your ferry pilots. I think they are moved to another sort of French Air Force somewhere else in Britain. It is so tantalising.'

9

Invasions

One day in 1942, I received a phone call from Air Vice-Marshal Musgrave-Whittam, the liaison officer between Organisation and the Air Staff, instructing me to go to an address near St James Square. There, using a special password he gave me, I would be admitted to a conference. I was to listen, and only to speak when I was called on to answer a question. I asked what kind of questions I might have to deal with. He told me to look up data on the weather across the Bay of Biscay in the autumn and particularly to note on how many consecutive days one might be able to fly aircraft to Gibraltar.

Along I went and after much security-checking I found myself in a conference room crowded with high-ranking officers of every service, both British and American. I had never seen so many admirals, generals and air marshals, and their American counterparts, together in one place. I found a seat at the bottom of the conference table, half hidden by a pillar, and sat there, fascinated by the business that unfolded.

The conference went in detail through the scenario of a great war invasion and fighting along the north

coast of Africa from Casablanca to Tunisia. After what
seemed hours the chairman reached the last item on
the agenda, Administration. 'Administration,' he quer-
ied. 'Isn't that all in order - shipping arranged, naval
plans made and so on?'

Up rose Musgrave-Whittam. 'Sir,' he said. 'there are
details of the air plan which ought to be reviewed. The
plan envisages flying some 1,200 aircraft from Britain
to assault Morocco and Algeria. Most of the these will
have to stage at Gibraltar, and many will be fighters
led by escorts. This is in itself a major flying operation
and will require considerable organisation. It is not
easy to fly aircraft across the Bay of Biscay. To be sure
of weather which will permit several consecutive days
of flying will affect both the plan and the date. I have
here an officer who is experienced in these matters
and I think you should hear from him before we
confirm the final arrangements for the invasion. Foss,
where are you?'

My tummy did a rat-tat-ti-tat as I arose from behind
the pillar at the foot of the table. Musgrave-Whittam
started to question me as though he were a pros-
ecuting counsel. 'How many days consecutively could
you be sure to fly fighter aircraft, following a leader
and inexperienced in this sort of operation, across the
Bay of Biscay in, say September or the following
months?' I gave the figures I had, based on our
reinforcement flights, which were made by inexperienced crews on their first overseas flight but who had
a wireless operator and a navigator. The data showed
that October and November were better months than
September.

Next question: 'In order to be ready to launch such an operation, how many airfields would you need for holding the aircraft, to give them the best chance and shortest flight to reach the Mediterranean?' I well knew that there were nine airfields in Cornwall and Devon, the nearest to Gibraltar. For more than a year I had waged a running battle on behalf of our small unit lodged on a Coastal Command airfield at Portreath, Cornwall, from which they despatched overseas two or three aircraft a night. This number was rising and our landlords considered us a cuckoo in the nest and were constantly encouraging me to find somewhere else to lodge.

My reply to Musgrave-Whittam's question was, 'We will need the full facilities of nine airfields down there.' At once Fighter Command's representative was on his feet: 'How can we defend such a concentration of aircraft if our bases are taken away from us?' Coastal Command followed: 'How can we cover the convoys...?' At the end of a hot exchange, Musgrave-Whittam said, 'You see, gentlemen, this is not easy to resolve. New priorities will be needed if we are to meet the plan and get air support safely into the theatre of war.'

I hurried back to my office in Bush House and went straight to my chief, Air Vice-Marshal Hollinghurst, Director General of Organisation (DGO). Holly was a magnificent staff officer, with a large department, preparing, planning and ordering all the manning, stores and other needs for the future of the war. He had to live a year or more ahead of the current phase of the fighting. It always seemed to me he hated the

sight of me coming through his door; so often I
represented an aircraft in flight and needing a decision
here and now, with few facts or background for that
decision. He said, as usual, 'Can't you see I'm busy? I
replied, 'Sir, they are going to invade North Africa in
two months. I've just been to a conference with Air
Vice-Marshal Musgrave-Whittam. They've placed the
responsibility for getting 1,200 aircraft out there
squarely on your department.'

Holly seized his telephone. 'Can you scramble?' he
said, and pressed the button that made the conversation secret. He swore, and I overheard Musgrave-
Whittam's Lancashire voice and laugh as he said, 'So
Foss has reached you, has he?' When Holly put the
phone down he said, 'Well, don't just stand there, get
on with it, it's your job.' 'No, sir,' I replied. 'I can either
do this job or the job I do at present. I can't do
both.'Holly thought for a few moments, then said,
'What about X? (an officer senior to me, whose office
happened to be next to mine). If you can help him,
I'm sure he could do it.' It was an admirable choice.

Very quickly the nine airfields in the south west
were commandeered, their telephones and communications completely revamped, their present inhabitants moved away or required to find footholds in the
surrounding fields. Shortly afterwards, Americans by
the thousands were arriving, to find what a beautiful
part of England the south west is. As history records,
the invasion went in and the majority of the aircraft
reached their destinations. But it happened nearly two
months after the original planned date. The invasion
took place on my twenty-ninth birthday.

These adventures in the Air Ministry confirmed my growing conviction that the RAF, and all the services, needed an enlargement of vision about air transport and its key role in the war and in the future peace. We were entering an era when aerial mobility would become a decisive factor in global warfare and in keeping peace in the world. Our small branch in Organisation had no hope of thinking ahead or of presenting policies; we were running as fast as we could to keep up with demands, and still being overtaken. However, events were forcing the authorities to arrive at the same conclusion.

One day, a civil servant asked me over to Air Staff. I found him drafting a policy paper for the Cabinet on the next stage in air transport in the Air Ministry, and the means to carry it out - RAF Transport Command. Needless to say I was delighted to give him my convictions, born out of experience, about the need for just such a central, unified, adequate authority. The War Cabinet adopted much of the policy paper.

Not long afterwards, in March 1943, the Directorate of Air Transport Operations (DATO) in the Air Staff was created to develop all aspects of RAF air transport operations. So my office, ADO (F), was wound up and at the same time a new command, RAF Transport Command, began to execute the directions of DATO and the Air Ministry. I was appointed to be Group Captain (Operations) of the new command with the Acting rank of Group Captain on 23 March. For about half a day I was, in fact, in command of the Command, until the new Air Officer Commanding, Air Chief

Marshal Sir Frederick Bowhill, flew in from Canada,
Ferry Command, Montreal.

He settled himself at my desk in my small office in
Bush House and said, 'Well, Foss what shall we do
first?' To which I politely replied, 'Try to find a
headquarters, sir, where both of us can sit down.' We
took an Air Ministry car out to Harrow to look over
an empty headquarters building and agreed to start
off there. About a month later I made a count of the
officers in our headquarters canteen and found eight-
five present, doing what four officers and six civil
servants had been trying to do thirty days earlier. One
year later I noted that our headquarters had around
seven hundred working in it. It was a measure of the
rapid expansion of air transport and its role in the war.

In order to carry out its function, Transport Comm-
and had to pioneer a new concept of command
structure: men and aircraft, wherever they might be
in the world, operated to the orders of a central
headquarters in Britain. Hitherto, if you went to India,
or anywhere else overseas, you came under the comm-
and of the local operational commander and fought
the battles he was fighting. You were on his strength,
to go where he decided, and you were accommodated,
rationed and clothed by him. From now on with
Transport Command personnel and its aircraft, units
and groups remained together and responded to
Transport Command's directions. They looked to the
local commander for defence, accommodation, rations,
supplies and support, but it was Transport Command
who appointed and promoted. It was usual for the
units in a particular command to be delegated to the

local commander for the support of his operations, but only as part of a world plan which Transport Command had agreed to with the local Command and with Air Ministry.

This concept did not immediately capture the enthusiasm of the overseas local commanders and their staffs. We had to fight some doughty battles to convince them. As a result, our local Transport Command commanders had a very difficult task to reconcile their two masters. But in Bowhill, our Air Officer Commanding, we had the most senior Air Marshal, and when he entered the fray other commanders became persuaded.

One of the earliest such battles took place when we operated the Liberator Flight from ADO (F) branch on the route from UK to Gibraltar - Cairo - Karachi (then in India). Each aircraft flew a shuttle out and back on a definite schedule, stopping for just an hour or two and changing crews. The load of passengers, stores and mail selected by the priority board at each Command HQ, was awaiting our shuttle, which left without delay. The round trip took less than a week, and Lyneham (Wilts) maintenance was set up like a civilian airline to keep the schedule. One day, one of our Liberators, due to leave Karachi, did not set out on schedule. Our signal to AHQ India received a vague reply that the aircraft was being held 'for a vital local reason.' When we got the aircraft back forty-eight hours late, we learned that a notable officer of no great seniority had not been able to join the aircraft on time. He had had some sporting matter to attend to, and AHQ had held our aircraft. It took 1425 Flight Lyneham nearly a month to get the schedules back to normal.

So the big issue became - who decided when an aircraft flew or was delayed? My ultimate chief, Sir Christopher Courtenay, the Air Member for Supply and Organisation, was prevailed upon to make it wholly clear that not even a commander-in-chief or a viceroy could delay a Transport Command air service without first consulting the Air Ministry.

One day in Command Headquarters a copy telegram came to my desk, sent from the local HQ in Calcutta, violently protesting a directive which I, as the Operations Officer, had given. The message was personal to our Air Officer Commanding, making it clear that I had crossed the wishes of that local commander. I dug out the file and checked that my signal had been both correct and diplomatic. Bowhill soon sounded his buzzer for me and I went along to his office. He had massive eyebrows and we reckoned we could read the portents by their position - high meant storms ahead, low meant all was friendly. Today I noted that they registered a mid-position. 'Have you seen this signal, Foss?' he asked. 'What is the story?' I explained and showed him my signal. He meditated for a moment and then said, 'It is very hot in Calcutta. Leave it to me to reply.'

Bowhill taught me many similar lessons. Here are two: the Senior Air Staff Officer (SASO) at Transport Command was Air Commodore Brackley, a former pilot and a manager of Imperial Airways, the pioneering national airline, today known as British Airways. He

was a very skilled and experienced operator of transport aircraft, particularly in the airline business. He
was never so happy as when he had a Meteor fore-
caster beside him, a pilot on one telephone and a flying
control on another, as they thrashed out the route, the
flight plan and the decision whether or not to fly.
Routes were more crucial in those days, before cabins
were pressurised or transport aircraft had oxygen, and
when even the Liberator came close to its maximum
range westbound across the Atlantic, because of pre-
vailing winds and gales.

Brackley did not relish policy papers and staff work
to the same degree. In fact, he undertook the tasks
normally performed by the Group Captain (Operations) - which was me. With my Air Ministry experience and Staff College training, I was better fitted for
the policy and paperwork. So, without anything ever
being said, we reversed roles. I dealt with the memo-
randa, papers and the working conferences that the
SASO would normally deal with, while Brackley was
in the Operations room or out on an airfield operating
aircraft.

One day Bowhill sent for me to ask my view on a
new air route he was considering. I made my suggestions and finished by saying, 'Of course, this is really
for SASO to give his opinion, but I've had no chance
to talk it over with him.' Bowhill said with a twinkle,
'SASO is busy with special flights. I think you are the
man to talk this over with, and you will deal with the
policies concerned.' I realised then that Bowhill was
well aware of our reversed roles and was pragmatic
enough to let it continue.

As I worked with Bowhill, I learnt more about his wisdom in handling people. One notable example occurred towards the end of the war in Europe, when decisions had to be made about the rapid transfer of forces for the assault on Japan. This was a task which would require an urgent and massive expansion of Transport Command, both in the routes to be planned across the world and in the numbers of squadrons and units. A major conference was scheduled to deal with this agenda, and Bowhill asked me to accompany him to it. Before we left, he said, 'I will meet the staff this afternoon to work out our tactics.' At this meeting we went over the plans, estimates and figures which our branches had prepared. They amounted to the re-shaping of the Command. As we were discussing estimates of the manpower we would need, Bowhill said, 'That is all fine, but what are we prepared to concede?' 'Concede, sir?' asked one officer, echoing the surprise we all felt. 'Yes,' Bowhill responded. 'Is there any one item that might be delayed, should that become necessary?'

At the impressive conference to which we went, Bowhill's strategy emerged. Gathered there were senior officers from each of the Commands, as well as senior Air Ministry officials. In turn each Command outlined its estimates of its personnel requirements. Before they were finished, it became clear that there were not enough men in the Air Force for everyone's needs. I could see that if Transport Command was to have the minimum we needed to train for and carry out this big new assignment, others would have to trim their requests. As Bowhill outlined what Transport Command required, some officers behaved as though they felt threatened by our expansion and by our very senior Air Marshal. I could detect some hard breathing among other Air Marshals, and some voiced their opinion that 'non-operational' was less important than 'operational' - fighting with guns and bombs.

At that point, Bowhill gave me a look and addressed the conference. 'Gentlemen,' he said, 'these arguments of yours are important, and I fully appreciate all that you have been saying. None the less, I must stress our essential requirements.' He paused and looked at the papers in his hand. 'However,' he continued, 'as I study our figures again, I wonder if we could delay item ten?' (One of our requirements for manpower.) His offer reminded me of the story of a Russian troika pursued by wolves, when the driver threw out one baby in order to save the others.

As we drove to HQ I said to Bowhill, 'I really don't know what was decided, sir, or which of our requirements we shall get.' 'Wait till you read the minutes of the meeting,' he replied, 'You will see that we've got what we asked for, but with item ten delayed, though agreed in principle.' And so it came about.

Another conference dealing with delicate matters, at which Bowhill summoned me to join him, was a luncheon meeting with the Directors of BOAC in a London hotel. I was not a stranger to BOAC. During my time in the Air Ministry I was appointed to be an RAF representative on the Board that co-ordinated civil aviation activities with the RAF. I used to attend weekly meetings with Wing Commander Rex Vaughan, the head of our Movements Branch, a part

of Equipment, who was also Chairman of the Priorities
Committee for air transport loads and passengers.
Vaughan was a barrister and a judge and an extremely
valuable man to have with me in that high flying
company on that Board. It included the Directors of
British Overseas Airways, the Permanent Under--
Secretary of the Air Ministry, equally senior civil
servants from the Foreign Office and other branches
of Government. Its Chairman was Captain Harold
Balfour, MP, Under-Secretary of State for the Air
Ministry. We who represented the RAF were given no
specific instructions, apart from a warning not to agree
to anything without first consulting our chiefs. Our
contribution to the deliberations was more often than
not a Russian-style 'No'.

It seemed to me that much of the time of this august
body was taken up with inappropriate detail. We
discussed the one or two trips a week made by the
BOAC Clipper flying boats between America and
Britain via the middle Atlantic and Lisbon. I don't
recall our ever getting around to the BOAC service
between South Africa, the Middle East and beyond.
We solemnly thrashed out whether valve-scaling on
engines should be done in Baltimore, Lisbon or Poole
- a matter, I thought, better decided by BOAC's Chief
Engineer. I suspected that these meetings were a
means by which these men kept abreast of what was
happening in our wartime operations and what the
prospects might be for civilian aviation in the future.
They could thus get their bids in ahead of any
competitors. When the issue arose of the RAF operating air transport services to the Middle East and

beyond, some real heat was generated. The Directors were totally opposed, even though the flying was through war zones. However, the Cabinet ruled against them, and Transport Command emerged to do the job.

As I left with Bowhill to attend the BOAC conference, he said to me, 'You'll get a nice lunch, so be friendly at the meal. Once we move to business, don't intrude at all, unless I invite you to. Listen carefully to what is said.' An excellent luncheon was served in a private room, though it was clear to me that I was not welcome. When it came time for business, hard negotiating about facilities and equipment required by BOAC took place. On the drive back to HQ, Bowhill said nothing about the conference, nor did he ever tell me why he had taken me to it. But I am certain his purpose was to ensure that I could support his remembrance of what was agreed, should anything different be attributed to him.

10

Three to Three Thousand

As each new stage of the war developed, Transport Command reflected its growth in size and complexity. It forced the armed services to re-evaluate the role of our Command. As concrete planning developed for the invasion of continental Europe, the role of Transport Command was very substantially enlarged by the inclusion of a hitherto independent No. 38 Group, under our Command. This Group was responsible for carrying and supporting the Army airborne forces. As a result, some 200 Dakotas (C-47s), aircraft used for training and lifting the airborne forces, were placed under our direction.

This addition involved a considerable shift in our thinking in Operations. Until then we had been mainly concentrating on our airline, ferrying and reinforcement roles. Now we had to consider a dual role for these Dakotas: first, the lifting of the troops and their equipment, the towing of their gliders with men and heavy equipment - even tanks; second, the load carrying possibilities, using the Dakotas like lorries. We had to plan for an increased number of personnel over and above the aircrew who would be needed to lift, haul and tie down loads in the aircraft; then to manhandle the loads out on parachutes or unload after landing in a combat area. We also had to plan an ambulance role for Dakotas; some aircraft were fitted for stretchers for their return flights from combat areas. Nurses needed special training and unloading points had to be located close to hospitals set up for particular types of casualties - burns, eyes and gunshot wounds.

Very shortly we discovered that these dual roles were not easy bedfellows. Once we began using the Dakota as a lorry, the Army started relying on its supply carrying. However, in preparation for an airborne drop, all the Dakotas had to be grounded for several days, while loads were readied, troops assembled and practised, equipment fitted. Meanwhile the generals were deciding when, where and if the operation would take place. Such a decision could change from hour to hour as the tides of battle swirled and new intelligence arrived. While this was going on, anguished cries mounted from the 'Q' (supply) side of the Army and the Royal Army Service Corps for re-supply of their stocks needed to keep the ground forces advancing to support the airborne. Some of these supplies were formidably heavy - ammunition and petrol, for example.

The Arnhem operation well illustrates the problems we encountered. After the armies had come ashore in Normandy, they had fought their way past Paris and northwards into Holland until the British reached Eindhoven. All this fighting had been supported by supplies brought into the temporary Mulberry harbours in Normandy and then carried by lorries over

broken-up roads. Now that distance was 400 miles and
the RASC had reached the limit of their capacity. The
great need was for a port closer to the battlefield, but
the Germans had left garrisons to defend all the port
towns. Now our Dakotas were delivering 2,000 tons a
day to Brussels airport.

The sight of three great bridges undamaged and
carrying a road into Germany from Holland must have
been a tempting sight for our highest command. If we
captured them, the war might be shortened by many
months. I suspect the Germans had not destroyed the
bridges because their forward troops needed this line
of supply. An airborne attack was called for to seize
the three bridges. The Americans were to take the first
two, and the British the most advanced one at Arnhem.

We had only enough Dakotas to lift in the Airborne
Division in waves over a two-day period. The airborne
troops, though highly trained, were very lightly
armed. When they found a German tank division
waiting near their landing area, they were forced into
a perimeter on the edge of Arnhem. Transport Comm-
and was then ordered to drop supplies into this
perimeter, an area not well defined for the over-flying
aircraft. This was a highly hazardous operation, not
only because the area was poorly marked, with no
communication between ground and air, but primarily
because of the presence of both German fighter aircraft
and flak guns.

In order to drop supplies with any accuracy, our
Dakotas had to fly straight and level at about 600 feet
to allow the Army Despatchers in the cabin to push
out the panniers of stores on their parachutes. It was

much like driving grouse over a moor for hunters to shoot them down. The pilots flew in their unarmed aircraft with amazing gallantry, but very few landed their stores within the perimeter. In six days of operation we lost about seventy-five Dakotas, and many more damaged and out of action for days or weeks.

At Command HQ we were beside ourselves trying to get the operation called off. It seemed to us such a lost cause, not worth the price in aircraft and crews, RAF and Army. At last it was stopped, and the Airborne were left to escape or be captured. I have long felt that the Army despatchers, pushing their heavy loads out from the dark tunnel of the cabin, never received adequate acknowledgement of their bravery. Equally, the nurses who tended the wounded in the air, flying off the Normandy beaches where they loaded under heavy shell fire, should have been particularly praised. And the same is true of the men and women who performed a similar job in Burma and on the China route. Out there, the advance of whole armies, such as the XIV Army which conquered Burma by crossing the mountains from India, was almost completely supplied by British and American Dakotas.

I had been very closely involved with the European invasion, not just operationally, but as a human spectator. I will never forget the days just before, during and after the landing on the Normandy beaches. I had been invited to Wiltshire to watch a mass drop of parachutists rehearsing for D-Day. I stood with an officer host on the edge of a field and heard the grumble of approaching engines. Suddenly the sky

filled with massed aircraft. From the lead aircraft a
body fell, without parachute, and disappeared behind
a hedge. A moment later, there was a cloud of
parachutes with swinging bodies, many with bags
hanging below them, filled with their stores and
heavier weapons. It was a beautiful and thrilling sight.

As we watched, down through the midst of the
descending men fell a man with his parachute only
half open - what the troops called a 'Roman Candle'.
As soon as the parachutists were on the ground, my
officer host and I jumped into a jeep and dashed across
the field to find the Roman Candle man. As we drove,
I shouted to my colleague, asking about the first
free-fall man. The Parachute officer replied, 'Don't
worry, we always give a body to the Gods to propitiate
them before each parachute jump. It's a dummy.' We
found our soldier, not dead as I fully expected, but
sitting on a tree stump, with his parachute laid across
his knees. He was a tiny fellow, very light in weight.
The Parachute officer slapped his back and asked,
'How are you, old chap?' 'I'm OK,' he replied, 'but I'd
like to meet the .... who packed this chute.'

As D-Day for the invasion dawned, I watched the
weather charts in our operations room at Transport
Command HQ. The high winds and low cloud over
the Channel made it look absolutely atrocious, both
for the airborne and the massed sea shipping. The
Allied Supreme Commander, General Eisenhower,
postponed the operation for up to forty-eight hours.
Beyond that, a postponement would have to be for a
month, to have the tides, moon and other conditions
right for the shore invasion - and all surprise would

be lost. Until this moment the Germans had been convinced that we would make a landing on the coast between Boulogne and Calais. Our counter-measures forces were doing everything they knew to keep up that pretence, but it could not last much longer.

Hour after hour on the day before the invasion and then for the next forty-eight hours, Air Commodore Brackley and I paced the operations room, the Meteorological office to scan the charts being drawn, and then the telex room to watch the messages coming in. The dreadful weather scarcely relented. Our hair stood on end with the stress. Then, after forty-eight hours, Eisenhower gave the order to go, a very courageous decision. 'Ike's mad,' said Brackley, as we thought of dropping parachutists in the dark under cloud and in wind speeds far greater than any they had jumped in by daylight. There were gliders to be towed and dropped so exactly that they could land inside the fort, with its coastal guns, by the beach where the British forces were to land. The gliders' mission was to capture the fort and prevent those guns from pulverising the landing craft.

Over our phones came word of the Dakotas taking off, one behind another, with the tow aircraft and gliders staggering into the air - a great armada. The landings and feats of that night are now history. I award the palm to those glider pilots who, under those ghastly conditions, found the forts and got down inside them, usually with a crashed glider around them. They captured the forts, just as others took the bridges and roads approaching the beaches, and made it possible for the landing craft to put their men and

vehicles ashore without such heavy casualties as we
had expected. Two days later, the engineers had
constructed a pierced-steel-plank runway behind the
beach and our first Dakotas were landing and taking
off with the wounded in minutes between bursts of
German artillery fire. Within the hour the wounded
were back in British hospitals and on the operating
table.

The Prime Minister took a continuing and detailed
interest in all the theatres of operations, but especially
the Middle East and later India. He kept a regular eye
on the build-up of aircraft, and our office in the Air
Ministry had to submit figures to him every week. I
received some probing queries. Once he noted that a
fighter, broken down half-way across the Chaddian
desert, in middle Africa, had not moved for a month.
I had to do a lot of chivvying to find out from Middle
East why it was there and how soon it would be
moving to the fighting front. Without that kind of
pushing, the aircraft could have lain there for years,
lost in the paperwork. But the Prime Minister's interest
got aircraft moving!
    Later, when the airborne operation to supply the
XIV Army's invasion of Burma reached its peak, the
Prime Minister probed into the statistics of the loads
hauled by British and American Dakotas. He noted
that although there were equal numbers of British and
American aircraft, the Americans were always carrying
a larger share of the 200,000 tons each month. He
wrote a firm note enquiring why. Nobody in England
could explain, and seemingly in India, either no one

understood, or they were too busy fighting the war to reply. So an officer was sent out to enquire. He found that when the next aircraft, British or American, was loaded, the total uplifted was recorded in 2,000 lb. tons. Back in Calcutta, clerks were busy dividing the half of the total load credited to the RAF into the heavier (2,240 lb.) long tons. So it was impossible for the RAF to equal the USAAF!

By 1944 RAF Transport Command had expanded into a huge operation with a world-wide outreach. I had reached a point where I was overwhelmed with the work and patently unfit to handle the job. Authority at last decided that the tasks of Group Captain, Operations, should be divided into three, and soon afterwards three Group Captains arrived to fill the posts. Unfortunately, none of them had had any previous experience of transport operations or their applications. So naturally they looked to me to brief them, but so did other whole areas of the expanding command HQ, since I had been the original officer, both in the Air Ministry and when the HQ office was opened. At this point Brackley came to my aid. He sent for me and said, 'Pat, the powers-that-be think we are going to liberate Holland and they want Princess Juliana brought over from Canada to ride her white horse in front of the liberating army. You know, and we all know, that we are likely to be stuck at Eindhoven for the winter, until a port is released to us. However, we are to send over AL 504 to Montreal to collect her. I want you to fly over with AL 504, have a good look around our unit in Montreal and the others we have inherited over there, have some dis-

cussions with the Canadians and occupy yourself for
a couple of weeks, then fly back on a delivery flight.
These Group Captains have simply got to learn to do
their jobs, instead of waiting on you.'

Liberator AL 504, captained by Air Commodore
'Taffy' Powell, took off from Northolt, west of London,
with a crew, myself, twenty ferry pilots returning to
Canada, another staff officer and our VIP, the Commander-in-Chief of the Canadian Air Force. When
evening came, the C in C rose from his seat and
addressed us in general, 'Have you guys ever seen an
Air Chief Marshal in pyjamas?' 'No, sir,' we chorused.
'Well, you're going to see one now,' he said, and
prepared himself for sleep in a fine bed in a curtained
area at the rear of the cabin. Powell then offered me
a bunk in the crew compartment and I went fast
asleep. Sometime in the middle of the night I awoke
in my eyrie close to the ceiling, looked down and saw
Powell and his co-pilot asleep below me. My reaction
was, 'Here we are, somewhere half way across the
Atlantic, and who on earth is up front in charge of the
aircraft?'

I jumped down, went forward and found in the
pilot's seat the Flight Engineer, chatting to one of the
ferry pilots beside him. Ten thousand feet below, the
Atlantic shone in the moonlight. The auto-pilot was
holding the Liberator level and on course. Behind the
pilot sat the navigator working some new-fangled
radar gadget which was fixing his position every
minute or two. He was checking its reliability by taking
star sights with a sextant and calculating from these
our position. He showed me our precise position on

the map, three-quarters of the way across. This was a
new world of navigation which AL 504 was pioneering, as she toiled along at 160 mph, against the wind,
with no pressurisation in cabin or cockpit, which
limited our cruising height to below 12,000 feet, the
comfortable oxygen limit. I thought, there's a considerable difference here from my experience, just ten
years ago, flying half frozen in the Vickers Virginia,
with its open cockpit, trying to spot remembered
terrain!

We landed at Ottawa, to put down the Air Chief
Marshal, after nineteen hours of flying. We still had
enough fuel to have gone on to Calgary, another 1,500
miles. In fact, this was the first-ever flight from London
to Ottawa. Then we flew back to Montreal and I made
my visits, going as far west as Lake Superior. Finally,
I flew back in a Liberator bomber being delivered to
the Middle East. We flew via Bermuda, then diverted
to Labrador, then to the Azores (Lagens), thence to
Morocco, where I left the plane and joined a BOAC
Liberator flying to UK. I'd seen a lot and learned a lot,
but most of all the journey had been a wonderful
respite from months of overwork.

Before this break, any time spent away from Headquarters had been just as busy. For example, towards
the end of 1943 Bowhill led a planning staff to India
to survey and prepare the air routes for the moves of
our forces to the Pacific for the war with Japan. We
flew in a Hudson with the minimum of comfort and
visited thirty-one stations and landing grounds in
thirty days, a desperately tiring routine. At each stop
we examined the facilities so that we could compare

them with our planned requirements, to make the fly-out swift and safe. Then at each Command we held a conference on how improvements might be implemented.

The chief Planner at Transport Command was Group Captain Dismore, who had been with me in ADO (F) Air Ministry as a civilian and had been a senior man in Imperial Airways. His assistant was Major R. Hilary, a Territorial Army Officer who had also been an executive at Imperial Airways. Although Hilary had been offered higher RAF rank, he resolutely refused to give up his Rifle Brigade rank and standing. Wherever we landed on our Indian survey, people would ask me, 'Who is the Pongo (soldier) and what's he doing with your lot?' My reply was, 'Wait and see when the planning starts.' Hilary was outstanding; he had done an enormous amount of work on the detailed requirements and plans for each stage of the route - the hundreds of thousands of gallons of petrol needed at each point, the numbers of beds, blankets and thousands of other items. No one could fault his figures.

At each conference we opened our presentation to Commanders with, 'The war in Europe will end on 1st April 1945.' Time and again we were stopped by the chairman asking, 'How do you know the war will end then?' 'That is the plan,' we replied. These men had a right to look sceptical; viewed from the Middle East, Gulf or India, at that time, the war was a succession of disasters - the relentless advance of the Japanese, the lack of men and supplies and a sense of no end in sight. On our side, we could have supported our statement with estimates of enemy attrition in Europe, invasion plans, the vast input beginning from the USA. Of course, our figure was wrong, but not by much; the war in Europe ended on 6 May 1945.

On my return from Canada, I was posted to command a new unit, the School of Air Transport at Netheravon, on Salisbury Plain. Nothing better could have happened to me. It was an opportunity to advance the cause closest to my heart, because the purpose of the school was to train officers, who were being moved from fighting Commands to Transport, in the ways of operating and managing a new concept of flying. Some thirty-five officers at a time, between the ranks of Wing Commander and Flight Lieutenant were to come for a three weeks' course. My aim was to change profoundly their whole way of thinking, to give them a new language and new attitudes before they were sent away to small distant units which had to work together over considerable distances, and often in a none too friendly environment created by local commanders.

My title was The Commandant, and my staff and I were responsible for creating the unit, working out its syllabus and developing its functions. Second in command was the Chief Instructor, a magnificent officer named Wing Commander Bill Coles, who had once been a policeman and had the physique of one. He was the only man I ever met who had won a DSO, DFC, AFC, and American DFC - all on unarmed transport aircraft. He had flown hundreds of miles behind the German lines in the Western Desert to land

and supply long distance penetration groups, to pick up and put down people and stores. He had performed similar operations in Burma with the Chindits, and he had led a squadron over Arnhem to drop supplies there. He was a great leader of men. Before he retired from the RAF, many years later, he had become an Air Marshal and gained a Knighthood.

Along with him, the School had a fine group of lecturers and course leaders, RAF and Army, a good group of airmen and airwomen who made the School function, and, very important, a station commander who was sympathetic and encouraging. Alongside the School was stationed an Air Transport Development Unit which experimented with the equipment which Transport Command used, from parachutes to tie-downs to anchor freight. Also on the station was a large parachute packing unit, whose function was to maintain and pack the parachutes of the operational airborne Divisions, for men and for equipment.

Our first task, at the beginning of each course, was to change the anathema men felt towards being 'non-operational', which they considered air transport to be, as opposed to 'operational', which meant action directly against the enemy. We had to convince them that the next phase of the war would be mobile - air mobile, as important as direct combat. We started by 'blinding them with science'. We described the current world- span of operations and what might lie ahead; the island-hopping in the Pacific, fought by the Americans and Australians against the Japanese, something few of our students knew anything about; the airlift into China, which enabled the Chinese to keep fighting; the support of the ground forces in the field, particularly in Burma. This panorama provoked thought and made men realise there was much more to this war than the little bit in which they had been involved. Then we set out to teach a jargon, a new concept of management and a loyalty to this new Command, whose units were scattered around the world, but who all answered to the central HQ.

I gave a talk on 'The spirit behind the Command,' in which I told stories to illustrate what made a good transport pilot and what did not. I gave as an example of the latter a pilot who flew a twin-engine aircraft, with a load of ferry pilots, above a ridge of the Atlas Mountains in North Africa. Suddenly one engine stopped. The ferry pilots chewed their finger tips as the aircraft staggered its way above the evil looking peaks. Then the engine came on again, and as the passengers were sighing their relief, the other engine stopped. It started up again and the aircraft made a landing at Ras el Mar. As the pilot pushed his way through his passengers, they angrily accosted him: 'What went wrong? Why didn't you tell us what was happening?' He replied jauntily, 'What's all the fuss? I always practise my one-engined flying on this stage.'

By the end of the war, in July 1945, some 300 officers had passed through the School, among them several senior officers who came for short indoctrination courses. One fall-out from these months happened a couple of years later, when I was flying a light aircraft from the UK to southern Africa. A chain of friends who had been students at the School helped me on my way down the continent. A more significant by-product

was that for the first time RAF officers began considering air transport as a function of an Air Force and a
normal part of warfare.

At the School we tried to lay a systematic foundation for the study of air transport, especially in time
of war. We collected material for textbooks, wrote
papers, went out to lecture, tried to interest the Staff
College and other centres of military learning. I was
determined that through this kind of education never
again would there be uninformed political decisions
about air transport, such as the one taken in the Middle
East to withdraw our few air transport units and
convert them into bombers, which were then lost over
Greece in an endeavour to halt the German invasion.
The outcome of that decision was that it held up the
British tanks poised to advance westwards across the
desert to Tripoli. They were denied the airborne
supply of fuel, stores, ammunition and spares which
they needed. One result was that the coast was closed
to our ships, the French in North Africa did not rally
to help us, and supplies and reinforcements had to be
shipped around South Africa. Thousands of lives were
needlessly lost and the war was probably lengthened
by a year or more.

That political decision was made at the highest
level. I take leave to suggest that there was no one at
that level who had any understanding of airborne
supply or, if so, the conviction to fight for its development. It evidently crossed no one's mind to fly appropriate aircraft into the area, to support a tank thrust
and change the whole Mediterranean situation.

What makes the matter even more ironic is that the German Luftwaffe had already demonstrated to our High Command the impact of large forces of transport aircraft flying in parachutists, troops and equipment, not only during the invasion of Norway and Holland, but much earlier, in the Spanish Civil War. As a Staff College student in 1942 I recall questioning visiting lecturers about how much we had learnt from the mistakes made by the Germans as they expanded their forces, so that we did not have to make the same mistakes. One lecturer on the subject of building airfields and stations replied very heatedly to that question, 'We do not choose to study the enemy or the mistakes they make.' This was greeted with hoots of laughter from my fellow students, most of whom had just come from fighting the Germans and had a considerable respect for them.

I was invited to lecture to the Institute of Transport in London in 1945. This body dominated the thinking on all aspects of transport - at sea, on land, under-ground and in the air. I gave a lecture on the subject of 'Military Air Transport', which was subsequently published. They evidently liked it, because they made me an Associate member and then awarded me the 1945/46 White Smith and Bristol Aerial Transport Medal for the best contribution to the science of air transport in that year.

At the close of the year I was also made an officer of the Order of the British Empire (OBE) by the King for services during the war.

11

African Encounters

I was thirty-two when the war ended, and very
unwell, probably due to the stresses I had experienced
and the responsibilities I had carried. I had started the
war with the lowest medical category. In the course
of six years I had taken a total of about one month of
leave. Many of my weeks were seven working days.
As I left the service to revert to the reserve in March
1946, the doctor advised a change and a complete
break. First, I had to go to Bournemouth to supervise
the re-opening of our family hotel, Linden Hall Hydro,
much damaged by its military occupants, until my
brother Denis could return from Australia. He was an
officer in a supply ship based there which had accom-
panied our fleet north, right into Yokohama harbour
for the signing of the Japanese surrender.

The hotel had been requisitioned early in the war.
Mother supervised the clearing out in a few days. She
had managed the hotel for twenty-one years - it must
have been hard for her. She moved to Cheshire for
much of the war. At the end of the war she joined
with her brother, Uncle Leo, and Aunt Queen Exton,
to buy a house in London. They undertook the

business of separating the Linden Hall hotel from the Exton Hotels group and the raising of the finance to allow Denis and me to get it open and operating by the summer. They gave us great encouragement and help. Meanwhile Hannen was still in the Army, being demobilised soon after. His part in the opening was to prepare the publicity.

Once Denis and his wife Nancy were back and managing the hotel I travelled to Caux, Switzerland, to assist at an international conference which was bringing together former enemies, including French and Germans, to consider the formidable economic and human problems of the war-torn areas of the world. I met delegates from countries in Africa and Asia, which were now to get their freedom from colonial rule, sitting together with former rulers to plan for their independent futures. The conference was run by my friends of the Oxford Group, with whom I had had my life-changing encounter ten years earlier. The Oxford Group was now known around the world as Moral Re-Armament. During the time of frantic military arming before the outbreak of war, Frank Buchman, the initiator of the movement, had called for a moral and spiritual re-arming of the democracies if they were to match the totalitarian might of Hitler. The phrase had caught the attention of the press and public. Now, following the war, the need to answer the hate and fear let loose in the world was obvious. My imagination was stirred by what I saw at the conference, although my own next steps were by no means clear.

With the approach of winter, my doctor again emphas-
ised that I must get out of Britain to avoid the winter
if I was to survive. I wanted to do more than survive.
I noted that many wartime friends were now looking
back wistfully at the comradeships, opportunities and
challenges of wartime which peace did not offer them
and dwelling on memories of those fulfilling years. I
wanted to look forward, grateful for what I had
experienced, but anticipating fresh challenges. It was
clear to me that the war of arms had not ensured a
peaceful world where men and women and nations
and continents would automatically get along well
together. As one of my friends put it, we were involved
in a war of ideas, probably as intense and unknown
as the war of arms had been. I was casting around to
see what my part and my place might be.

The place soon clarified. During the war I had
helped entertain Cyril Pearce, a South African businessman on a purchasing mission in England. He had
talked about Africa and its future, a continent which
interested me. When I told him of my hope to visit
Africa after the war he had said, 'If you ever get to
Johannesburg, come and stay with me for as long as
you like.'

During the autumn I toyed with the idea of buying
from the surplus stores a light military plane, an
Auster, used by the Army as a spotter plane, and to
fly it to Africa. I talked the idea over with a friend,
whom I had come to know well through Moral
Re-Armament, a Scotsman named Charles Burns.
Burns was a former regular Cavalry officer who had
been thrown from a horse and had broken his neck.

Despite having to walk with two sticks and being in frail health, he insisted that he would go to South Africa with me. He had made thorough enquiries about travelling there. He learned that only priority passengers were being accepted by the airlines and shipping companies.

In November 1946 I was in London, talking with Frank Buchman and other friends about future plans now that the war had ended. A propos of nothing that had gone before, Frank suddenly asked, 'Who is going to South Africa?' I said, 'I am, Frank.' 'Would you consider taking Andrew Strang with you?' he asked.

Andrew Strang was a Scot whom I had known before the war. He had recently been repatriated from a German prisoner-of-war camp, where he had spent the war after being picked up as a civilian in Denmark, when Germany invaded that country. My first reaction was, 'That man must weigh all of 180 pounds; I'd never get an Auster off the ground with the three of us.'

Charles and I phoned Andrew and invited him to fly with us to South Africa. We heard him gasp. He told us his sister in South Africa had invited him to come there so that she could nurse him back to health. Like Burns, he had been discouraged by the travel difficulties. He was delighted at the idea of flying with us. And I discovered that Andrew, thanks to the prison camp, now weighed far less than 180 pounds. Charles and he put their heads together and came up with an offer to buy, not a war surplus plane, but a new aircraft.

I found the first post-war production Percival Proctor III for sale at Luton, north of London. It was a four-seat, low wing monoplane, made of wood, with a Gipsy VI engine. Painted white and blue, it looked beautiful to me, especially when the registration letters, G-AIYZ, were painted on its sides. I collected it on 21 December and flew it to Bournemouth. There I gave it a check flight to confirm the petrol consumption, the compass and so on. All was well, except that I had a doubt about the accuracy of the compass. However, the weather closed in and we had to stay on the ground. We spread our maps over the floor of the hotel ballroom and cut them into strips. We made a pack-up of spares, including a tyre, then found we could have only twelve pounds each for personal baggage. We packed the rest of our clothes and sent them by sea to Cape Town. On New Year's Day, 1947, we took off from Bournemouth, to fly to Bordeaux, in southern France, on the first stage of what proved to be an unforgettable flight.

After three cold and miserable days in Bordeaux, with the weather impossible for flying, we took advantage of a slight break to take off for the Mediterranean coast and Nice. We climbed between the Pyrenees and the Massif Central until ahead of us we saw mounting masses of cloud. I tried to fly over the top hoping to arrive over the Mediterranean and then to descend over the sea. In hindsight it was foolhardy, with no radio. We had had great difficulty in translating the weather reports in French so they were of little help.

We reached a height where the Proctor was struggling. There were dense and ugly clouds below us and towering all around us. Andrew announced he thought he had seen the sea below us. I turned the aircraft to look and cut into the edge of a towering cloud. Our wings' leading edges quickly covered with ice, and chunks of it flew off the propeller blades. The aircraft wallowed, out of control, and we plunged into the clouds. In a dark brown half-light we fell about as I sought to get the Proctor into a steady glide. Golf ball sized lumps of ice were forming on the petrol tank vents and I feared that they might stop the petrol flow to the engine. Then suddenly I saw a tree pass by us standing out of snow, then more trees. We were gliding down parallel to the slope of a mountain. By the grace of God we were pointed in exactly the right direction and there were no outcrops to collide with. Suddenly we plunged out of the bottom of 10/10 clouds into a steep-sided valley about two or three miles wide.

The valley floor was deep in snow and the clouds were solid from wall to wall. I turned south and followed a railway line. Passing over a little town, we read Langogne on the railway station boards. We could not find this name on our strip map - it was off it to the north. We flew on south until the railway dived into a tunnel. I made a dicey turn in the valley and flew back to Langogne. The only possible landing place was a football field. We landed safely and tied the Proctor down.

At that moment a party of Frenchmen arrived. Andrew struggled to talk to them in French and in the process uttered a few German words. One of the men broke into German; he had just returned from a German prisoner-of-war camp. When they heard of Andrew's prison exploits, nothing was too much trouble for them. They led us to a small hotel, where we joined them in their Twelfth Night celebrations. In the morning I found that I could get the petrol we needed at an airfield at Le Puy, 40 kilometres to the north. There was much discussion in the bar about getting me there. A truck driver offered to take me at an outrageous price, then a man offered to do it for nothing. He proved to be the local tailor. Next morning he and his young son drew up at our hotel in an ancient car. In the back I noted spades, rope and planks. I quickly learned why they were there. Soon we were digging our way through six-foot snow drifts. Other motorists joined us in the digging. It took us six hours to get to our petrol and we had to spend the night at Le Puy.

The only way I felt we could get the Proctor off the football field was to strip it down and send Charles and Andrew on by train. Off came the wheel spats and everything that did not affect airworthiness, our baggage and spares. Charles took this collection to Nîmes, just south of the mountains and where I expected to land. Andrew was to see me off, and then take the train to Nice, our original destination on the Mediterranean.

A group of high school children had come to the football field to see the take-off and the priest in charge asked me how they might help. I asked them to stamp down the snow in a diagonal across the field and post youths fifty metres apart along the path. It was a brilliant day with no wind. I ran up the engine and then made more than one dash, but each time lost my nerve and braked. Finally, I asked two brave souls to sit behind the tail, holding back the tail wheel while I ran the engine up to full, then released the brakes. The Proctor became airborne at the edge of the field, where it sloped into a railway cutting. One wing brushed a small fir tree, smashing a headlamp glass. I sank into the cutting, slowly climbed out of it and circled to gain height to cross the mountains to the south.

While I was attempting to get off the field, the priest approached Andrew, who was getting more and more worried, and asked him what more they could do. 'Please pray for my friend,' said Andrew. The priest gathered those not assisting me and led them in prayer. Later he told Andrew that the last plane to land in that field had been a German during the war. They had not prayed for him and he and his companions had been killed taking off.

As I topped the last range I saw the southern plains covered in fog. I tried to fly below it, but it was down to the ground, so I turned back to Langogne. There I saw I had sufficient fuel to fly to Le Puy and I landed there. Andrew saw me circle the town and head in the direction of Le Puy and followed me there by train. Meanwhile poor Charles in Nîmes was desperately trying to get through on the phone to stop me from heading into the fog. Then he set off on his two sticks and with all this unwieldly baggage to travel by train to Marseilles and Nice. He caught up with us the following day.

With more delays through weather and engine troubles we flew on via Corsica, Sardinia, Tunis, Malta, Castel Benito and Benghasi, then along the North African coast to Egypt. After a stop with friends in

Alexandria and Cairo we headed down the Nile, across the Sudan and into Uganda and Kenya, making eight stops on the way.

Some incidents remain in my mind. In Nice, held up by bad weather, Charles and Andrew decided that we needed more cash than the twenty English pounds we possessed. Charles phoned the Consulate and talked with an honorary consul, probably a local businessman, who advised him to use the black market, where his pounds would fetch many more francs. Charles objected and the consul cut him off.

Charles and Andrew found out that the Consulate was open until four o'clock. They started walking towards town to catch a tram. After a mile they had not the strength to go on further and sat down on a bench. After a few minutes Andrew said all he could think about was a white bus. Charles felt assured that all would be well. After some minutes, down the road rolled a white bus, which pulled up, and they climbed in. They didn't know whether the driver understood their poor French, but in the middle of town he stopped in front of a building and waved for them to descend. On the door a sign proclaimed 'H.M. Britannic Consulate'. It was ten to four. My friends sat in a waiting room. A man walked by them and Andrew sprang from his chair. 'You're Z, aren't you? We were in Camp XXX together.' 'Andrew! My old friend! You helped me escape from that hell hole. What are you doing here?' Very shortly cheques were cashed and that evening we had a delightful dinner with the official.

On the flight from Cagliari in Sardinia to Tunis, about 130 miles of sea crossing, the weather was stormy and the clouds ahead looked almost black. I climbed through layers of broken cloud until I found a stratum of steady air. Below, the sea was whipped up into white horses, with no ships to be seen. My imagination began whirling about how I could ditch in the rough water if we had an engine failure. Our only flotation aid was a small inflatable ring on which Charles sat.

Suddenly I heard an unusual noise - an irregular clicking. My eyes scanned the gauges - all steady as a rock, the motor purring sweetly. Andrew was looking at me with alarm. Then we both looked over our shoulders, to see Charles, sitting among the boxes, banging away on his tiny typewriter. He claimed that this was the first time the aircraft had been steady enough for him to catch up on his correspondence. From Malta we intended to fly south to Tripoli over 250 miles of sea, a good two hours of flying. As we were running up the engine prior to take-off an RAF friend climbed up the wing to speak into my ear. 'I say, old man, would you take this suitcase to Tripoli?' I replied that I was sorry, but we were really loaded to the gills. He put his mouth closer to my ear and whispered, 'It's a dinghy, old man. If you come down in the drink, get in it and we'll find you, never fear. Hand it to the Controller at Castel Benito and I'll collect it.' It went alongside Charles in the back.

We flew steadily southwards for two hours and up came the coast of Africa. Immediately ahead was a small headland, with desert stretching away in both directions. In the hazy air I could make out no distinctive landmarks to fix our position on our small scale map. In such a situation the professional method is to work out a search - taking the remaining flying time before you run out of fuel, you deduct ten minutes for a reserve and divide the remaining time by three. This allowed us to fly along the coast for about twelve minutes, then back again and fly in the other direction for the same time. Which way to turn first?

As we circled the headland, I explained the procedure to my friends. We were quiet for a minute, then each of us in turn said he felt we should turn east. We did so, for twelve minutes, seeing nothing identifiable along the coast. So we turned back to the headland and continued west for another twelve minutes. Still we could see nothing. I said, 'We must look for somewhere to put down.' I had barely spoken, when out of the murk houses appeared and then the port of Tripoli. Had we first flown twelve minutes west and turned, we would probably have had to force-land some sixty miles into the desert - three unfit men with no way to tell the world where we were. When I handed the dinghy to the Controller at Castel Benito, he said, 'You took rather a long time on your trip, didn't you?' I agreed with him.

At Khartoum, in the Sudan, we ran into a seemingly insuperable obstacle to our onward flight. A government order forbade any aircraft not equipped with radio to fly south alone. This was the result of a retired General flying himself to Kenya before the war and having to land in the Sudd, the huge area of swamp between Malakal and Juba. The efforts to find and rescue him had unbalanced the Sudan's annual budget. Hence the prohibition. An airline captain offered for ten pounds to say he was escorting us. However, with his speed and height we would have been out of sight of each other in minutes, and he did not land at Kosti, where I needed to refuel. I feared I might be grounded there.

I made enquiries as to who made decisions in such matters and learnt that it was the Director of Civil Aviation. A new one had just been appointed, and when I heard his name I was pretty sure he had been a student of mine at the School of Air Transport. I rang him and introduced myself and he was pleased to hear from me. I told him my problem and that I was not prepared to bribe. He hummed and hahed. He was, he said, new to his post and to the country. In the end, he said, 'Just this once - tomorrow I will be in my office, staring at the wall and asking no questions. Please be out of the Sudan in twenty-four hours and for God's sake don't do anything like getting lost.'

At first light we were airborne for Kosti, then Malakal and then Juba. It was our longest flying day of the trip, and had its problems. The Notice to Airmen gave this warning about Malakal: 'Airmen are advised when landing or taking off at dawn or dusk to keep a sharp lookout for elephants who sometimes obstruct the runway.' The hundred or more miles of Sudd, with its tall, waving grass above marshes, without a distinguishing feature except an occasional vertical glimpse of a waterway, together with smoke from large areas of burning grass, made navigation difficult, and we were afraid we might miss Juba. We found it and were grateful to find beds in a rough and ready hotel. But at dusk drummers started to beat a rhythm, repeated loud and steady through the entire night, making sleep impossible.

Between Kisumu, on the north of Lake Victoria, and Nairobi we crossed the mighty Rift Valley, a 2,000-foot deep slash across the face of Africa, starting at the Dead Sea in Jordan and continuing to near the Zambesi in southern Africa. We flew above volcanoes, spewing smoke or steam, and approached the sheer wall of the Valley. I set the Proctor to climb, but although I pointed our nose up, the aircraft sank and the ridge rose higher above us. My insides tightened and I made ready to turn away. The air through which we were flying was sinking, then suddenly, when it seemed we were bound to fly into the cliff, the mass of air lifted us several hundred feet above the summit and we descended to Nairobi. We arrived on 1 February 1947.

We remained in Kenya for two weeks, making some lasting friendships. We were able to help people who had been divided by the war and by disagreements on beliefs to forgive and to be forgiven. It was an encouraging experience and the prelude to seven years of living and working in Kenya, during which I became engaged to be married and where later our son Andrew was born. In after years we still returned for visits, as Kenya became a second home to us.

For the moment, however, we pressed on to South Africa. I decided to fly down the coast through Mozambique (then Portuguese East Africa), reckoning that I would be less likely to get lost and that there would be beaches and cultivation on which I could force-land if necessary. Flying over the sea was also more comfortable than over Kenya and Tanganyika, where I had encountered huge bumps in the air - very uncomfortable for passengers and for myself, prone to feeling sick, even when at the controls.

When we reached Lourenco Marques (now called Maputo) near the southern border of Mozambique, we turned west and flew inland to Johannesburg. In the late afternoon we passed by mountains and above a high plain. It was very hazy, the sun was a red ball sinking in the west. We kept seeing hills of white and yellow, not marked on our map. Later, I learnt that they were spoil dumps from gold mines. Feeling lost, I still kept steadily on course until Andrew said suddenly, 'There's a line of aircraft on the ground below us.' I said, 'We'll go down there and apologise later to the Rand Airport.' The Johannesburg Rand Airport was the official Customs and Immigration port for all incoming flights. As we taxied past the control tower I saw on its side 'Rand Airport'.

Friends made us welcome in Johannesburg and later we flew on to Cape Town, visiting Andrew's sister en route. As we relaxed in the Cape we began to realise that we were on more than a trip of a few months to recuperate. We were there to play a part in Africa's future.

In 1949 we welcomed to Cape Town a large group who brought the play, *The Forgotten Factor*, by Alan Thornhill, a drama of industrial and family life. It was received with acclaim when presented in Cape Town.

I travelled up to Johannesburg, South Africa's largest city, to prepare for the production's visit and to
find a theatre. I learnt that the open sesame in that
city was the approval of the Chamber of Mines or one
of the mining companies. I do not recall how I
achieved it but I found myself being ushered into the
office of the Chairman of the Chamber of Mines, a Mr
C.S. McLean. I tried to present in the most positive of
terms the play and its message of building unity
between classes and between management and labour.

As I was speaking, Mr McLean interrupted and said,
'Do I understand that your group are advocating a
get-together between management and the workers?'
'In essence, yes, sir,' I said. 'What do you know about
1922?' he asked. I replied, 'I am sorry. I don't know
anything about 1922.' 'Well, I suggest you ask people
in Johannesburg about 1922,' he commented. 'If your
play and your group are here to suggest that management and labour ought to get together, then we'll have
nothing to do with it. Management is here to manage.
We give the best possible conditions you will find
anywhere and if people don't like them, then let them
go and try somewhere else.'

A few minutes later I found myself down in the
street and feeling as if I had had a heavy kick in the
back. My friends, 1,100 miles away, were counting on
my producing a theatre in Johannesburg and here was
I closing every door along the gold reef towns. At that
moment, down the street through the milling crowds,
came a gentleman wandering along. His face was
familiar, but totally unexpected in a city where I knew
scarcely anyone. He saw me and greeted me warmly.

Then he said, 'You do not look very well.' He was François Leger, a Frenchman whom I had met in Caux. We had fried 750 eggs together in the kitchen, a memorable feat since neither of us had ever cooked an egg before.

I told my friend of the interview and my feelings of being crushed. He shrewdly said, 'We have patrons like that in France,' and then added, 'In Caux, when we did not know what to do, we used to pause and listen to God. Let us do that now.' So there in that crowded street we stood and paused. As we did so, I had a good feeling that out of this defeat wonderful things would follow.

How François came to be walking in that street seeing the sights just at that moment is a remarkable story in itself. He had married a South African lady and they lived in France. They had had a grim war. After the war he applied to take his family to South Africa and had been refused until they discovered that, in fact, he had been born in Oxford, England, while his mother was hurryingback to France. He had arrived in South Africa only a few days before.

And what of 1922? In that year there was a great strike of white mine workers. It concluded with military action, with the Army sent to put down the miners besieged in a mine complex. Artillery was used and a number of lives lost. There was a great bitterness at the way the management had won, which lasted for years.

After many enquiries I discovered that a producer who had booked the small Municipal Theatre for the week that we wanted was having difficulty in getting his show ready. He passed the theatre booking to us. On the first night we played to a well-filled house, mostly brought by our friends. I was manning the office we used as a box office and on the second day an African messenger appeared and requested six seats together for his boss. I had not got six seats together, so I regretted and he went away. Soon after, the phone rang and a voice said, 'I sent a messenger round for six seats. My friend, you will have to find those seats. They are wanted by the Chairman of the Chamber of Mines.' I persuaded others to re-arrange and sent the seats round.

Mr and Mrs McLean came. They invited the cast to a reception in their home. Why did this change happen? Apparently, in the first night audience was a group of students which included the McLean daughter. We can only guess what she must have said to her parents. It was enough to bring them to see the play.

In Durban we played to a mixed race audience for the first time, something absolutely new for South Africa in a public place of entertainment. As ours was not a strictly commercial production, the audiences were by invitation. We had invited all races, without realising the risks we were taking. In came the crowds and just sat themselves down. No one commented and the only reaction we noted was thunderous applause from all parts of the house.

The cast circled South Africa with the play, in theatres, African halls and schools. Then it went to Rhodesia and to Northern Rhodesia; finally to East Africa.

In many of these places they were presenting a live dramatic performance for the first time ever. In some halls an Introducer was used who explained the salient points of the play in the local vernacular before the performance in English. Though many could not understand English, or only a little, we were amazed to see with what understanding and intense interest they followed the show. They lived into every episode. It took our cast a while to acclimatise to certain African reactions. In one scene the trade unionist's wife bursts into tears at the first sign of affection her husband has shown to her for years. This was a moment when Western audiences might cry. Not so the Africans; they burst into laughter - which quite threw the actress playing the part on the first occasion. It was explained to us that this was the African way of releasing emotion and showing appreciation.

In one Central Africa town we built a stage with empty beer crates, set up curtains and lights, rehearsed and then brought in the audience. It was packed and the atmosphere was of excited anticipation. The introduction music was played and then our electricians turned up the lights for the opening scene. Immediately all our lights went out and so did almost all the lights in the town. Our switch-on had been the final straw to break the camel's back of a hopelessly overloaded town system.

The local military rushed in a portable generator and coupled it in and the show restarted. The generator went with us throughout the rest of our tour in that country. We did notice that it was we who were the only surprised people at the cut-off!

My cousin, Valerie Exton, who was an important
member of the cast and production team, was taken
severely ill with asthma just before the cast left for
Rhodesia and the north. She was hurried into the huge
General Hospital in Johannesburg where she lay in a
ward of asthma patients all struggling to breathe. She
had been sharing a room with Margaret Ogilvie,
another member of the cast and the mainstay of our
box office. Each day I drove Margaret to the hospital.
I realised that it was Margaret's striving to keep up
Valerie's morale that kept her alive from day to day,
while patients died around her. I began to want to
know more about Margaret and to appreciate her.

Year by year, in my mind, I had compiled a list of
the virtues a girl would need before I would propose
marriage to her. Each year the list had grown longer.
While Margaret visited Valerie I had an hour to wait.
One day I went for a walk in the Zoo Park. Suddenly
as I walked along I had a clear sense of God speaking
to me. It was as real as if a voice had spoken. 'This list
of yours - there is no girl in the world who will come
up to your list. You must take whom I choose.' Then,
'Margaret is for you'.

When, some minutes later, I picked up Margaret at
the hospital I looked at her with new eyes.

My uncle and aunt, Leo and Queen Exton, with my
mother, soon arrived in South Africa as we got Valerie
out of that ward. Margaret was with us as Valerie
recuperated in a house on the seashore at Hermanus
in the Cape.

I flew off to Kenya to the farm of Jack and Esther
Hopcraft in Njoro with the intention of working there

and getting really fit while I considered the future and marriage. After six months I flew to England to see my mother and also Margaret's parents. They all encouraged me. Her father, a Scot, a wonderful man with a delightful sense of humour said, 'Whatever Margaret decides I will support her to the end.' Her mother was clearly for it.

So back to Kenya I flew and arrived just as the cast was gathering at the Njoro farm to prepare for the Kenya tour. Friends had come there from all over Kenya to help launch the show.

The Forgotten Factor was advertised to open in a week in Nanyuki, in the north of Kenya, before moving to Nairobi. The scenery, lights, costumes, etc. were in Mombasa docks, 500 miles away. I hurried down to Mombasa to arrange the importation. Forty-eight hours before I had been in harsh cold and ice-bound scenery in Britain. Now I was sweltering in damp heat. In Mombasa everyone assured me that I had no hope of getting anything just arrived through the port before they shut down for a week for Christmas. There was an enormous backlog and no way to cut the corners.

I walked for miles questioning people. I found our boxes in a shed. I discussed with the railmen how, if I got them released, they could get the boxes to Nanyuki quickly. I began to learn how the whole importation system worked. Finally, I found myself in an office of an Indian clerk. In front of him was a tray piled high with papers; it looked at least two feet high. Slowly, he was taking off one sheet from the top, examining it, then stamping it before he put it in the 'out' tray.

He was glad to stop and chat. He explained to me that these were the key documents, the bills of lading, and this great pile in front of him was all bills of lading waiting to be processed, first by him. Until his stamp was on the document nothing could be done elsewhere in the port. He told me it took about six weeks to get a bill from the bottom to the top of the pile. We talked on and had an orangeade together.

I asked him how far our bill of lading might have got up the pile. He searched and finally found it. After examining the bill he suddenly stamped it and put it in the 'out' tray. I looked amazed and then warmly thanked him. He replied, 'Nobody ever comes to Mombasa to see me and hear how my job goes.' Sometimes people phoned and cursed him. If he thought the matter was urgent enough he might search for and pull out a bill, but not often. For MRA he was glad to do it. We shook hands and I promised him tickets for his family when the show came to Mombasa, which it did. I offered to carry the bill to the further offices, acting as his messenger. Our cargo got through the port and up the railway before the shut-down.

I travelled back the 500 miles to the Njoro farm to find a very busy group of people. I was able to tell them the good news. Then I had the opportunity to propose to Margaret. Without hesitation she said 'yes' which was a joy to me and to everybody there. I was thirty-eight and Margaret thirty-one. We had a six months' engagement during which mutual understanding and love grew in a wonderful way, as both of us took time to learn about each other, good and bad.

In June 1952 we were married in a lovely pre--Norman church at Herstmonceux, Sussex, with three hundred guests. The sun blazed and the whole function went through superbly.

12

Mau Mau

In 1947 Jomo Kenyatta, a Kikuyu political leader who later became the founding president of Kenya, returned after fourteen years in exile in Britain and Russia. Huge crowds gathered to cheer him at every railway halt between Mombasa and Nairobi. It was a hero's return.

The white people were divided about how to receive Kenyatta. I recall one occasion, attended by the Minister of Health, Sir Charles Mortimer, a man I respected, when Kenyatta was invited to speak on building black/white relations. A good deal of froth had been spouted by the preceding speakers. Kenyatta started by describing his feelings when, coming to this meeting, he found himself followed by two Special Branch detectives, who were listening to him even now as he spoke. 'Sooner or later,' he said, 'they will arrest me and send me away into the northern desert.' People there tut-tutted, but he spoke of what he knew.

Sitting one night at dinner with another guest who was a distinguished white citizen of the country, he began to talk venomously about Kenyatta. I suggested to him that 'every word you have said will be in

Githenguri by morning'. Githenguri was Kenyatta's
home and the centre of his independent school system
which reached all over the Kikuyu country. He replied, 'Of course not, this is a private house.' I
commented that the servants were all Kikuyu. 'They
do not speak English,' he said. 'That may be,' I
answered, 'but I did notice that they seemed very
attentive to what you had to say as they served the
meal.'

He went on to observe that if he had his way
Kenyatta would be shot like a mad dog. I suggested
that in England that would be considered to be murder
and I asked him how Kenya judges would react to it.
'Our judges understand,' he said. 'We can fix it.' 'That
is a most interesting thing to say to a visiting Englishman,' I responded, 'since we used to be proud that
British justice was incorruptible.' He was angry and
confused. He tried to recall his remark and assured me
I had quite misunderstood.

Our visiting group was invited to Githenguri by
Kenyatta and was joined by several white Kenya
settler farmers. Kenyatta assembled many hundreds of
school children. They listened to our quartet sing
'When I point my finger at my neighbour, there are
three more pointing back at me' and other songs. With
big visual aids we told them about moral values and
how to live a life of service for the nation. We watched
the children march past.

Kenyatta appeared to be delighted with the group.
He gave us the impression that he was open to a
friendly approach by anyone who sought to do their
best for the country.

In my view this was an opportunity lost by the government of that day. They could, if they had been brave and far-sighted, have encouraged Kenyatta to play a part in the policy-making in the legislative assembly. There was already one black member, Eliud Mathu. Policy and government were carried out by British civil servants and they gave an impression of still living in the regime of pre-1939 and the war. To have taken such a decision would have meant not only a change of personal attitudes but also bucking a coterie of white and brown Kenyans who were vociferously opposed to the advancement of the black. They by no means represented the opinion of all whites and specially those who had been away to the war and fought with black troops. But they talked as if they spoke for all.

Among Kenya men who guided us around were two clergymen of the Church Missionary Society (CMS), both of whom had a rare accomplishment in speaking fluent Kikuyu. Most white persons learned the lingua franca, Swahili, for general communication. There were many tribal dialects and languages, and also Asian languages, hence the need of Swahili. Unfortunately most people only acquired enough Swahili to shop, work, buy and sell, and exchange pleasantries. When it came to discussing deep issues, like what idea a man might have in his head, both sides ran out of Swahili.

Our friends took us to visit mission stations and to meet their friends among the Kikuyu. These kept telling us about a secret society called Mau Mau which was capturing the thinking of many younger people, and more often the high school and other intellectual youth. The Mau Mau's strength was in the secret oaths people took which bound them to obedience in a very sinister way, even when the oath was taken under duress. It seemed to us that a lot of the Mau Mau ceremonial was lifted directly from Christian prayer books, and their songs adapted from church hymns. These were re-written to make a Black God the king of Mau Mau, and the Kikuyu peoples the paramount tribe of Kenya and of Africa. This would follow as an intervention of God if the people did exactly what they were instructed to do. At that time authority seemed to know little about the extent and aims of this secret movement. We heard almost no mention of it.

Some friends invited a leading member of the Legislative Council to dinner to tell him what we had learnt about Mau Mau and to suggest ideas of how it could be countered with ideas and people being different. He started to listen and then he said, 'Tell me, how long have you been in this country?' 'About six months,' we said. 'I have lived here all my life,' he commented. 'When you have lived here as long as I have, I shall be interested in your opinions.' He was several years older than any of us so we could never catch him up!

It was in 1952 that MRA brought the play *The Forgotten Factor* to Nairobi and played it to multi-racial audiences. Among the hundreds who thronged the performances was a young African, David Waruhiu, one of the first black District Officers in the country. He was a Kikuyu but stationed in the Wakamba country. His father was the Senior Chief of the Kikuyu of the southern part, the area immediately north of Nairobi and extending up to the 14,000-foot Aberdare Mountains. The population was about 400,000.

David was challenged by the play and came along for a talk. He listened to God and was clearly told to do three things. First, he went to the Wakamba Chiefs and confessed that he had used his position to make money from the rationed sugar distribution. He promised to put it straight and that there would be no more corruption in his work. Second, he apologised to his wife for despising her because she had little education (which was the case with the majority of Kikuyu women at that time). Finally, he went to his father and apologised for his critical attitude towards his stepmother.

The Senior Chief took a dramatic step. He summoned the men of his area and spoke to them about Mau Mau. The police said there were 40,000 men there. He declared Mau Mau to be evil on two counts: first, because it gave oaths in secret, and sometimes under duress, and in the dark. That was contrary to Kikuyu way of life and custom, he said. Second, because Mau Mau was anti-Christ and he and many there were Christians. 'Wherever you find this beast, drive it out of the thickets and into the open air. It will never live in the open air,' he was reported as saying. He invited all the men to take off their hats (a mark of adulthood) and take an oath with him to drive out the Mau Mau wherever it might be found. Sitting on the platform behind him were men known to be leaders of Mau Mau. It was a very brave thing to do.

Shortly after, the Chief was driving along a road when he saw a car broken down with an African driver. He stopped to enquire if they might help the driver. The man said, 'Are you Chief Waruhiu?' 'Yes,' said the Chief. The man produced a pistol and shot the Chief dead.

This murder precipitated the Government into declaring an Emergency. The Police and Army were instructed to rout out Mau Mau and put it down. Regrettably the Police had almost no Kikuyu in their ranks, and the Army likewise. Without Kikuyu speakers and knowledge of the tribe, information was difficult to get. They tended to take the line, and even more did the British Army, that a Kikuyu was Mau Mau until he could prove he was not. It closed doors all over Kikuyuland. The Police and Army found themselves chasing and fighting a will-o'-the-wisp enemy among an antagonised population who were very roughly treated. The war lasted three years.

In the years immediately preceding the outbreak of Mau Mau there had spread from Ruwanda, to the west of Uganda, a powerful Christian movement called Revival, or Bulokali. The Christian movement had spread through Africans right across Uganda and into Kenya. It had become quite a powerful movement among the Kikuyu.

When the Mau Mau were precipitated into war by the Government's declaration of an Emergency, which I believe was months before the Mau Mau leaders had intended, they had to get the loyalty and co-operation of the Kikuyu public, both in the reserves and on the European farms, as quickly as possible. The Mau Mau leadership decided to achieve this loyalty by ruthless actions not previously experienced by the inhabitants. The Bulokali were among those who refused to take Mau Mau oaths or to co-operate with them; indeed they posed an alternative idea. We were told, soon after the Emergency began, that around 1,200 Bulokali men and women had been put to death for refusing to take oaths, mostly strangled with fence wire or chopped with pangas (the cane-cutting knives). During all the Emergency less than one hundred white people were murdered. The majority of these were friends of the Africans, killed to break their relationship with their African workers or, in at least one case, buried alive as a sacrifice to the gods of the mountain.

One evening the Mau Mau went to a village, Lari, a few miles to the west and north of Nairobi. They decoyed the menfolk away and then fell upon the women and children. Some they burnt in their huts and others were chopped with pangas. Many died, but even more were alive when they were found and rushed to Nairobi Hospital. The Police and Army hurried to the village. Meanwhile forty miles away at Naivasha the Mau Mau overran the police station and prison, seized arms, released captured leaders and took away explosives. They were all gone by the time the military arrived.

Nairobi radio reported the Lari massacre and appealed for blood donors for the injured women and children. Within two hours a queue of all races stretched from the hospital doors.

That morning David Waruhiu came in great distress to the house where Margaret and I were staying.

He told us that no one in authority would trust a Kikuyu whoever he was, yet Mau Mau could not be contained and beaten without the full co-operation of the Kikuyu people. This he believed could be achieved especially if villages could be protected and defended by their own people. Unless decisions were taken quickly further Lari massacres would follow.

Telephone calls were made to Kenyan leaders with whom we had had some contact. Later that day we smuggled Waruhiu into the State House where Governor Sir Evelyn Baring asked him to talk to a meeting of the War Council. They gave David authority to go into the reserve and bring back one hundred men for whom he would stand guarantor. These men were to receive immediate training in weapons, and authority to go back and raise a force of defenders, a Home Guard, who in turn would be trained and armed by them. Within a year the Home Guard exceeded 17,000 and proved to be a major factor in not only defending villages but also in hunting the Mau Mau and limiting their supplies. They knew who were likely to be Mau Mau in a way the Army and Police could not.

We had made friends with a District Commissioner, 'Taxi' Lewis, at Kitale in the west. He had asked our help in sorting out some forestry workers who he had reason to believe contained Mau Mau elements. We took along a group of amateur actors, white and black, and we put on a show for the foresters. Our skits caused a lot of laughter. We talked with the men who seemed impressed with the sketches and the moral that they suggested. We had no idea whether our efforts had done any good, but Lewis seemed both pleased and convinced that they had. Shortly after, he was appointed Commissioner of Prisons and moved to Nairobi just before the Emergency began.

The first police action when an Emergency was announced was to round up all suspects of Mau Mau: the 'Jock Scott' operation. To the observer it looked as though they had rounded up all the Kikuyu trade union officials and intellectuals and any Kikuyu who had shown any political awareness, especially in municipal affairs. These men were trundled down to a camp at Kajiado, on the road south to Tanganyika, and there detained. 'Detained' meant that they had no sort of trial, no opportunity to defend themselves or even to find out what was the circumstance which had led the police to round them up. All they knew was that the Governor had signed a Detention Order with their name on it and they were in until the Governor chose to release them. For many this was years later.

At Kajiado they were housed in long low huts inside a high fence with barbed wire. It was in a dry desert and lions came sniffing around the wire in the night. As detainees, they were not asked to work, so most of the day they sat around talking and complaining about the lack of water, of food, of bedding and other essentials, as well as at having been put inside. The short notice given meant that the administrative services had been overwhelmed and the nearest town was over fifty miles of dirt road away.

Detaining these men seemed to have no obvious effect on the leadership of Mau Mau; just as the arrest and sentencing to seven years of Jomo Kenyatta and six other 'leaders of Mau Mau' also had no apparent effect.

It has long been good revolutionary tactics to have political sympathisers who may even think they are running the show, who are in the public eye and therefore the people the police pick up; but they are not in fact a part of the direction and do not know who is.

David Waruhiu and I visited Kajiado to talk with his friends inside the camp, among whom were some of the best educated brains of Kikuyuland, and see what could be done to make them useful citizens once more. We had long talks with them. Then that same evening I sat down and drafted a paper, in Staff College style, on how men like the ones we had seen in Kajiado might have their wrong ideas re-oriented and replaced by positive ones. In this way the detainees could become constructive and useful citizens once more. They could help to change the thinking of their peoples and build a new country. The paper was diplomatically couched and with a minimum of detail. By morning we had typed it out and delivered it to Lewis's home.

'Taxi' Lewis expressed interest in the idea of the paper and asked if I would help by recruiting suitable men who would take it on, and also if I would help with the re-orientation side. He had a new camp about to open at Athi River, about twenty miles east of Nairobi in a hot plain, and he proposed to devote it to the action suggested by my paper. He asked us not to advertise what we were doing so it would not be spiked before it had had a trial. It was a brave thing to do on his part for he was bound to be criticised for stepping out of line, where punishment and elimination was the tune rather than redeeming people. And he was heavily criticised in due time. But he encouraged us to go ahead.

I proposed Lieutenant-Colonel Alan Knight as the Camp Commandant. Alan had been an outstanding officer in training black troops in the war. He farmed at Kitale and had spent almost all his life in Kenya. He believed in the guidance of God and wanted to help these men to serve their country constructively. We selected Major Peter Anderson, a farmer at Nakuru, who had a fine war record in Ethiopia and Burma, as second-in-command, and he was taken on. We went around to a number of other farmers and persuaded them to come to the camp as officers.

What was now needed was men who could speak with the detainees in their own language and who understood their way of life and custom. We set out to find volunteers in Kikuyuland. David Waruhiu, the Revd Howard Church, fluent in Kikuyu, and myself drove off in a three-ton truck with six armed police in the back to drive from south to north of the Kikuyu country. Messages had been sent ahead and at each village where we stopped David would address the men who had come to volunteer. They would come forward and give us their names; then we would drive on.

At one famous mission we called on the Scottish clergyman. He said, 'I have heard what you have come for and I am all for it. But please do not take my headmasters.' We showed him the list of volunteers

from his area. Tears came to his eyes. On the list was
every one of his headmasters.

In the event Government decided that only twelve
Instructors might be recruited and a rate of pay was
fixed. It interested me that nowhere had a volunteer
ever asked us how much he would be paid or how his
family would be protected or looked after.

Without consultation with us the twelve were sent
off to a Further Education College, ostensibly for
instruction in the techniques they might use. A white
schoolmaster was put in charge of them. On their first
day David Waruhiu went to see them and asked if he
might address the party. He spoke in Kikuyu which
the official did not understand. Roughly what he said
was, 'This white man here has some obvious spiritual
problems. If you Instructors could get him on his
knees, asking God for forgiveness, and change him,
you will have qualified to do the same for the Mau
Mau detainees.' We heard only a few days later that
the white teacher had passed the men as qualified. At
the start the Athi River camp had some 800 detainees.
All these men (and a few women) were sent because,
in the opinion of the Governor of Kenya and his
advisers, they were beyond redemption. They were
graded 'Black'.

The camp consisted of a series of enclosures with high
wire around and watchtowers at the corners. In each
compound were long huts.

The first task Alan Knight had to do was to make
the camp secure, not only barbed wire to keep detainees in but also to prevent anything that might be

smuggled in or out. For example he discovered that one senior warder made a practice of letting out paying customers (through a fault in the fence) to visit a Masai village where the prostitutes flourished. The warder moved elsewhere. Another warder going off duty was searched at the gates and was found to be carrying a number of detainees' letters to post. One letter was addressed to a brothel manager in Nairobi (from the brothel's owner inside the camp) stating, 'This man is a friend of ours. See that he has a bottle of gin and a girl for the night.' This was persuasive stuff for the warders.

Day by day Alan drilled his warders, called Askaris, in full view of the compounds, until every man was standing tall, handling his weapon with skill, looking fit and proud of himself. Their wives came to watch the drill. Alan's view was that men proud of themselves were less likely to give way to corruption. It was not usual in prisons to train Askaris in this way. But it produced the result he looked for.

The detainees were entitled to a scale of food which the Prison Department calculated for men who are not doing manual work. The Askaris, under prison regulations, were paid a sum of money to provide themselves with rations. To buy food the Askari or his wife had to walk about four miles each way along a dusty road to get to the nearest Duka (shop), returning up hill. Almost none did this, we discovered. They ate food from the detainees' cookhouses and took it for their wives and families. The detainees complained they had not enough food. Authorities told the press that the scale was adequate and there were no grounds for this complaint. Alan arranged to open a Duka inside the camp manned by a warder's wife. Then he announced that anyone found taking detainees' food was 'for the high jump'. Grumbling noticeably diminished after that.

Alan had to sort out senior staff as well. One professional prison officer had come early to the camp and provided the only 'expertise' among the officers. Soon after Alan arrived the rumour reached him that there was an unsatisfactory relationship in this man's house. The rumour was all over the camp. Alan had to invite him to choose between sending away his cook's wife or moving on himself. After an uncomfortable twenty-four hours the officer decided he could not send her away. So he moved away to command another camp.

It needed a lot of courage to tackle moral issues like that, but on that foundation the work of reform had to be built.

The next big hurdle was how you got the detainees to break with their allegiance to Mau Mau and begin to work out with our Instructors and officers a new way of life. There was a solid resistance, a hatred that came at one like a black cloud. We had to find that first man who would break and decide to be different. How?

We talked it over many times with the Kikuyu Instructors. They knew many of the men in the camp and some were relatives. But they could not penetrate the wall of resistance which was pervasive.

After about six months a crunch point was reached. Up till this time the lavatory buckets in each compound were collected and emptied by men of another tribe. Alan now told the camp leaders that in future the buckets were to be emptied and cleaned by the detainees. On that day the detainees were paraded. They sat themselves on the ground and absolutely refused to tackle the buckets. The officers faced them; the Askaris manned the towers with their machine guns. The atmosphere was sultry and menacing. The sanitary lorry stood there awaiting its load. Alan gave the order and not one person moved. They sat and stared at the standing officers with hate-filled eyes. It seemed a very long pause.

Suddenly, and quite without any previous arrangement, one young white officer stepped forward, walked to the latrine house and appeared with a bucket behind his shoulder. He tipped it in the tank on the lorry, pulled some grass and cleaned it out. Then he set off to put it back. At that moment another white officer followed him and did the same. On the third trip a detainee suddenly got up and took the bucket from the officer and, in front of the whole camp, dumped it in the tank and cleaned it. There was a hiss and many scowls. But the three men went on until that latrine had been finished. Meanwhile, the detainees had had to sit in the hot sun watching it all.

The next day the camp spokesmen agreed that they would do their own buckets; indeed they wrote a song about Knight and his buckets which they sang as they drove round, and it caused a lot of laughter as the chore proceeded.

That one detainee was taken aside by the Instructors and they spent many hours talking with him. He made a confession that they wrote out and he put his thumb mark to it; a step that, if it had ever got into the hands of the police, would undoubtedly have led to his hanging. But, at the end of it all, he looked a totally different man with a sparkle in his eye and a lightness of step. He asked that he might go back into his compound as he hoped he might convince others to come and talk. He was warned of the retribution Mau Mau leaders might take on him. They worked out a system of signals if he needed quick help. It was a real risk and later some of the men who changed were injured before they could be rescued.

This first man brought to the wire several others whom the Instructors helped to be quite different. Those who chose to were put to work in a separate compound, creating vegetable patches using the waste water of the camp. The gardens blossomed, for the Kikuyu are good horticulturalists. This was added pressure on others to change. In two years some 600 men decided to give up their Mau Mau beliefs and ask for help in getting new ideas to construct a new country.

Alan could promise a detainee nothing if he changed. The best he could do was to move him into a compound where he could garden, once the Instructors had given their assurance that the man had really come clean. Until the Governor's 'Black' detention order was rescinded he had to stay in the camp. There were no signs of that happening. Indeed, there was criticism in the clubs and government circles of MRA getting into this camp.

One day a group of journalists arrived. They were blasé and aware of the criticisms of MRA working in the camp. They asked Alan, 'How do you know that these men are changed, that they are not fooling you in the hope of privileges or an early release?' His reply was, 'Go into the compounds. Talk to the men and have a good look at them. I think you will be able to tell who are the changed men and who are not, whatever they may say.' They went around the camp for a couple of hours. When they came back several said to Alan, 'You are right. You can pick out the men who have changed by their looks and behaviour. They ought to be released. They're useful citizens now.'

There was additional fury in 1955 when a visit was paid to Athi by a mission of 190 MRA visitors, drawn from many nations, which included diplomats, industrialists, trade union officials and some eminent actors and actresses who were performing the musical *The Vanishing Island* in the National Theatre. This was a part of a world tour with the play and they had just come from Cairo and Teheran and were en route to London.

From the prisoners' standpoint this visit was a major turning point in healing their bitterness and giving them hope. For the first time they had an opportunity to meet and talk with eminent people of many nations, to feel they were respected and connected with the outside world once again. But perhaps more important it provided an occasion for their Commandant, Alan, in front of his staff, visitors and camp assembled, to apologise for his attitude of superiority. He promised them that in the future he would work with all who decided to rebuild Kenya in the spirit of unity and faith in God.

At the time Alan was having additional difficulties because the detainees had been increased to around 1,000, also he had suddenly received 600 women convicts with their warders and wardresses. Prisoners and detainees have quite different regulations and regimes. It did not help to have these women cheek-by-jowl with the men. Criticism continued. A very simple issue seemed to bring it to a crescendo. Alan had been encouraging the detainees to write and produce plays and sketches. They delighted in play-acting and produced quite a high level of production, considering the difficulties. Nairobi officials came to see one show.

One sketch opened with a grocery shop with its black proprietor. A long queue was waiting to be served and at the head of the queue was a black clergyman - incidentally we had several clergymen among the detainees. As the curtains parted, up the line walked a white lady who appeared not to notice the queue. She proceeded to announce her require-ments. The grocer scurried about, climbed a ladder, and then she changed her mind once more. All the while the queue waited patiently. Finally, when her bag was heaped high, she turned to the clergyman and said, 'Boy, take that out to the car.' The detainee audience fell off their benches laughing. Mrs Church, the chaplain's wife, would not have played the part if she had not felt it was a fair comment.

The Nairobi officials were horrified. Alan shortly received a letter prohibiting any play-acting and pointing out that such a scene lowered the prestige of the British. They had wholly overlooked the fact that the sketch was written by a detainee, a black man, and everyone there knew it could be true to life. The white staff acting and laughing with them, could do nothing but good in building a new relationship. Soon after, Alan was notified that there had been a change of policy. The 'Athi methods' were considered inappropriate and unsuitable for general adoption. Therefore the camp would be closed and the staff dispersed back to their farms. Alan was awarded the MBE.

However, closing the camp did lead to the detainees being re-classified as 'Grey' and assimilated into the general rehabilitation scheme which led to release in a few months. At that time there were over 60,000 detainees who required thousands of Askaris to guard them; all the costs of feeding, housing and securing falling on the tax payer in Kenya and Britain. The 'Grey' man, or woman, had to be of good behaviour for so many months and then he was released to the supervision of his local Chief for further months. Soon the Kikuyu had achieved their pre-eminence and Independence followed.

Going back to Kenya eighteen years later, I found old Athi men in many top jobs. They greeted you like an old buddy - 'We were in Athi together', rather like having been at the same school. Values they had acquired there seemed to sway them still.

One other story I would like to tell of those days. At the MRA Assembly in Caux in 1952 were two Kikuyu

leaders. One was the editor of the Mau Mau newspaper. The other man was a close friend of Jomo
Kenyatta. They heard that the police had arrested him
in Kenya and charged him with managing Mau Mau,
along with five companions. My friends had to take a
decision about what they should do. The editor
decided to go to London and build a new life there. I
have kept friendship with him for over thirty years.
The other man decided he would return although he
well knew that he would be arrested and put on trial
with Kenyatta. He considered they might get several
years in prison but he felt that he had gained a spirit
at Caux that might help in that trial and imprisonment.
He flew to Nairobi and was arrested on landing. They
all got seven years to be followed by restriction to the
northern frontier province. Several of us tried to send
him news each month. I am convinced that this was
a help to him and Kenyatta to come out of prison
without great bitterness.

Kenyatta was restricted to Marsabit, a mountain on
the road from Kenya to Ethiopia. Two of our friends,
both former Mau Mau leaders, obtained permission to
fly up there with a projector and the film 'Freedom', a
full-length feature film made in Nigeria; written, acted
and produced by black men. Jomo endeavoured to
translate the film to some of the audience who did not
speak English.

At the end he said that this film must be shown to
his people all over the country, but it must be in a
language they could understand. The friends had been
planning for this and assured him it would be dubbed
in Swahili.

At that time I was helping with MRA Productions
in London, distributing films all over the world. We
got a message that the film was required in Swahili
and that these two men were coming to do it. They
were assisted by a white Kenyan girl secretary. It was
a major undertaking costing over £5,000. We sent word
to many friends and money began to come in. When
the two men were in London they went to see an
industrialist in the City.He listened to their story and
their passion for Kenya to start aright. As they left after
lunch a cheque for £5,000 was handed to them.

The men worked day and night, living with us in
our house, and within three months the film was
beautifully dubbed into Swahili - you simply could not
tell that the original characters had been talking
English.

The film was shown all over Kenya, and then
Uganda and Tanzania. One English car dealer raised
money to provide two mobile daylight film vans which
went from village to village with the film, driven by
three youths from Britain who volunteered to do it
and paid their own way out. It was estimated that over
one million saw the film around the time of Independence. A senior policeman gave as his opinion,
'One reason why Independence came peacefully and
without bloodshed was the impact and outreach of
that film'.

For two years of the Mau Mau emergency Margaret
and I lived in borrowed homes around Nairobi. Our
son Andrew was born there in 1953.

One night David Waruhiu came to dinner. Afterwards he went and sat with the house and garden

staff. When he returned he told us that he suspected
three of them of having taken Mau Mau oaths. He
thought they would give us no trouble until a gang
came into the area and demanded action. We had
inherited the staff with the house. Several had been
working there for over twenty years. I found it an
immensely difficult decision, complicated by the fact
that I had been asked to go to South Africa in a few
days, leaving the family behind. I could send the
servants home or just dismiss them. No one would
take on a Kikuyu servant if he was dismissed without
explanation. I was not clear that I should do that. I
had them all in and talked to them, saying I knew
certain of them had taken Mau Mau oaths - which
they all vehemently denied. I told them I had to go
away and leave behind my wife, baby and our Swiss
companion in their care. I was going to trust them to
see that they were not molested. I finished by saying,
if anything should happen to any of my family, I
would not cease from searching, for years if need be,
until I found them.

They cared for the family for several months while
I was away. More than once they were swept up in
Army and Police searches of the area for screening.
Each time they came back. But deep in my heart I was
pretty sure David Waruhiu knew the truth.

An RAF friend of mine was posted away from
Nairobi to Britain. We saw the family off at Nairobi
station. Just as the train began to move out he leant
out of the window and handed me a box, which I
found contained a small automatic pistol and ammunition. Reluctantly, Margaret wore this when working

around the house through the day. At nights, after we had locked and barred the windows and doors, we kept it by the bed. Almost every white person was carrying a gun at that time; indeed, I heard that more were killed and injured by gun accidents than ever Mau Mau murdered.

One day we were driving onto a friend's farm in the dark. Our headlights revealed monkeys in their vegetable garden raiding the fruit. I seized the gun from my wife, cocked it and tried to fire to scare them off. There was only a click, no bang. It did not work. In daylight we discovered that the gun's striker had been broken off. All the time we had carried it around it probably had been useless. The sight of it might have tempted some brigand to attack a lady to steal it. We handed it over to the Police.

*   *   *

Our seven years in Africa and our many visits since to that incredibly beautiful continent have been of untold worth to Margaret and me. The wide open spaces are matched by the wide open hearts of the African people. Their deep family loyalties, their love of their land, their courage and their humour mean so much to us. Their amazing ability to forgive and their generosity have been some of the most important lessons in our lives.

These experiences in Africa, so unexpected when we had set out, reinforced my faith which had grown through the war years when faced with unknown and sometimes dangerous situations. I learnt that trust and team work, when coupled with asking God to show what is right, make the toughest difficulties fade and bring people together in unexpected and amazing ways.

Index